WITHDRAWN FROM COLLECTION
OF SACRAMENTO PUBLIC LIBRARY

The IT Marketing Crash Course

How to Get Clients for Your Technology Business

Raj Khera

Copyright

The IT Marketing Crash Course:
How to Get Clients for Your Technology Business

Copyright © 2013 by Dheeraj (Raj) Khera.
All Rights Reserved.

ISBN-13: 978-1482714036
ISBN-10: 1482714035

Published by MailerMailer LLC, makers of Presstacular,
www.Presstacular.com - online marketing for technology
companies

Rockville, Maryland USA
Phone: +1-301-825-5658
www.ITMarketingCrashCourse.com

If you like this book...

I am hopeful that you will find the ideas and tips presented in this book useful for growing your technology business. I've included actionable steps at the end of each chapter.

If you like the book, I would be grateful if you posted a positive review on Amazon or on other book review sites. You can also reach me directly on LinkedIn - I would love to hear your feedback:

www.linkedin.com/in/rajkhera

Acknowledgements

I would like to thank Meg Rayford and Jean Miller who assisted me tremendously in editing this book and to Chelsea Rio who designed a spectacular cover. Your support was instrumental. Thank you!

About the Author

Raj Khera is co-founder and CEO of MailerMailer, an email marketing software company, which serves thousands of customers worldwide helping them generate warm leads and win new business.

Prior to MailerMailer, he co-founded GovCon in 1995, which he and his partners grew to be the largest business-to-government web portal and sold it in 1999 to a publicly traded company. He also runs MoreBusiness.com, cited by the *Wall Street Journal*, *Forbes* and others as one of the best websites for small businesses. MoreBusiness.com is visited by nearly 100,000 entrepreneurs every month and offers a wealth of free resources to help start and grow companies. Raj's personal blog is called *Creating Luck*, *www.creating-luck.com*.

Before starting his first business, Raj worked as a semiconductor electronics engineer at the National Institute of Standards and Technology near Washington, D.C.

He holds B.S. and M.S. degrees in electrical engineering from the University of Maryland, College Park and was a former president of the university's chapter of Eta Kappa Nu, the electrical engineering honors fraternity.

In 2012, he was appointed by Maryland Governor Martin O'Malley to the Maryland Economic Development Commission. He also serves on the Board of Visitors for the University of Maryland's College of Computer, Math and Natural Sciences and several other boards.

To Mira, Zak and Tripti

My daily dose of sunshine

This Isn't Really Just a Book

It feels like a book, but it's much more. It's a *marketing vehicle* that will accelerate your IT sales. You can turn the concepts you will learn about here into your personal marketing tool. And it doesn't stop with the last page.

This vehicle keeps moving you forward with new marketing trends, ideas, checklists, white papers, webinars, videos, case studies of other IT companies like yours, and more.

To access this additional wealth of information that is included with your purchase, register your book at:

www.ITMarketingCrashCourse.com

Don't skip this step – do it now before you forget!

A Quick Note...

When you read this book, you'll notice a few references to a product called Presstacular. It is an innovative product that we've developed to help IT consulting companies generate warm leads and win more business.

If you would like more details, please see the description at the end of the book in the Appendix. You can try it free at *www.presstacular.com*

Table of Contents

Part 1: On Your Mark

Part 2: Get Set

Part 3: Go

Appendix

PART 1

ON YOUR

MARK

1

Getting Very Clear on What You Sell

"Success demands singleness of purpose." - Vince Lombardi

There are Riches in Niches

The meeting room at the Hilton was packed. During a break, the guy sitting next to me leaned over to introduce himself. Since this is what networking is all about I was happy to make his acquaintance. You never know where these connections might lead.

I asked the standard question: "So, what does your business do?" His response left me confused, really confused.

"We perform IT services for government agencies, businesses, and nonprofits."

This was a pretty vague answer, so I dug deeper. He replied, "Things like web design, managed services, network management, and software development."

"So, how big is your firm?" I asked.

"We're relatively new. My partner and I work with several other folks to pull in expertise required for our various projects," he answered.

He might as well have said "I'm just starting out, I don't have any business, and I'll do anything to make a buck."

If I were a prospect for him, there is no chance I would ask for a bid from his company. Why? Because I want to hire experts, not generalists. Experts go deep into a topic. That allows them to ask questions that hone in on what I might need. Really good experts, the ones who have built a reputation for themselves, know all about a technical issue. They are able to illustrate options for solutions and explain trade-offs. Hiring a generalist might seem cheaper upfront, but their mile-wide, inch deep knowledge will likely overlook important considerations that can be very costly down the road.

Prospects Prefer Specialists, Not Generalists

Let's say you were looking to build a deck for your house. Would you prefer hiring a company that specialized in building decks, or a general contractor that did all sorts of construction projects? The deck company will have numerous pictures of decks they have completed. They can also offer best practices and answer questions about the pros and cons of the latest composite materials. A generalist doesn't have that level of depth.

When you focus on a specific area of IT consulting, you gain the ability to build a reputation for being the "go-to" source for that specialty. For example, there are so many Microsoft products that you can use for developing solutions. Each has its own purpose. A prospect who needs a SharePoint solution will find a SharePoint expert to be the better bet over someone who also offers web design services. While you may be technically adept at both, a prospect won't see it that way. From their perspective, they want a specialist. There is a level of comfort they get by knowing that their needs are being addressed by someone who really knows their stuff.

By developing a marketing message that is tuned into a niche, you can target prospects like a laser beam. Your messaging becomes very clear and your prospects become more comfortable with your capabilities. This means you have to pass on opportunities that aren't within your focus, regardless of your aptitude to offer all sorts of IT consulting services. When you are starting out, that can seem like a hard pill to swallow. Just think back to the deck builder for inspiration. Focusing on one specialty is important.

Focus Deeper, Pick One Audience

Let's say you picked managed services as your area of specialty. There are thousands of others who also offer managed services. Your competition could be one-person shops to well-managed, finely-tuned corporations. How can you differentiate yourself among so many choices that confuse your prospects?

You could say you offer better service. But everyone says that. Unless a prospect has hands-on experience working with you, or a trusted adviser has recommended your services, they have to rely on other factors to make their decision. So, now what?

Ed Mana, owner of Technology on Demand, a managed service provider (MSP) in New York, figured out the answer. There are many MSPs offering their services to all kinds of organizations. Their client bases include nonprofits, dentists, doctors, lawyers, and roster of other businesses. Not Ed's. He focuses on only one type of business: audio-visual companies. "There are riches in niches," Ed will tell you proudly.

Ed's extraordinary focus allows him to contact audio-visual companies (and there are a lot of them in New York) and say something nobody else can say - that he only provides managed services to audio-visual companies, so he has a much greater understanding of their needs than any other MSP. His competition is no longer the other thousands of MSPs knocking on their doors. It is only an MSP who also specializes in this niche, and there aren't many of those.

The Building Blocks of Your Expert Reputation

The conversation with prospects becomes very different when you speak their language. The services you may offer are similar to other companies, but all that is lost in the prospect's mind. They only care about themselves and how you can help them.

When they perceive that your services are designed just for companies like them, you create a bond. You are no longer just one of those other vendors adding clutter to the prospect's buying process. You are viewed as the expert. You start to build trust. And people buy from those they trust.

Picking your area of specialty and honing in on the audience you want to reach are the most critical steps in creating your marketing strategy. You need to know exactly what you offer so prospects don't get confused - remember, they are not necessarily technical experts. That's why they are looking to hire you for technical work. You also need to know exactly who you need to reach so you can craft your messaging appropriately.

I'll discuss how to construct the framework for your marketing messages in the next chapter on your buyer personas.

Checklist: Your Next Steps

At the end of each chapter, I will provide you with questions to get you thinking about the concepts I've covered and how you can apply them to your business. Use these checklists to be sure you are getting the most out of each chapter as you refine your marketing efforts.

- What audience could you serve that is being overlooked, or is currently underserved? Look in your local Yellow Pages to see how many listings there are for different types of industries for insight into market size and potential.

- How big is each potential niche that you identified? Roughly how many potential customers can you identify? Is the niche too narrow (i.e., not enough potential customers)?

- Does the client base in this niche have the budget to be able to afford your services? Don't chase companies that can't afford you - you'll be wasting your time and theirs.

- Do you have any unique capabilities that can provide this niche with tools or services that others cannot?

- What can you tweak in your product or service offering that would resonate with buyers in this niche?

- Do you have any connections to some of the companies within this niche that can serve as references or be profiled as case studies?

2

The Most Overlooked First Step in Marketing: Your Buyer Persona

"The aim of marketing is to know and understand the customer so well the product or service fits him and sells itself." - Peter Drucker

Who Exactly Buys Your Technical Services?

A general doesn't go into battle with guns blazing. There is careful and deliberate planning. Without basic research and well-thought-out scenarios, he could drain resources quickly.

Your battle plan needs to focus on the right strategy and messaging to reach potential buyers. That means your research needs to start with a clear understanding of your buyers' motivations. Why would they pick you over anybody else? You need a clear picture of who buys your products and services, their research and buying habits, the influencers that contribute to the final purchasing decision, and the market forces that can sway a buyer's timing.

What Makes Your Ideal Customer Buy What You Sell?

Jeff LoSapio was hired to help a company identify how their employees responded to a phishing attack. In the course of doing the project, he realized there were numerous scenarios that he needed to account for which weren't in the initial budget.

He saw an opportunity to turn this unsuccessful consulting project into a business. He could help many companies through a SaaS (software as a service) solution that simulates a phishing attack, monitors how employees react, and provides individual guidance on how to handle the threat. ThreatSim was born.

To make sure he didn't spend his marketing dollars trying to reach the wrong prospects, Jeff created a detailed profile of his ideal client, often referred to in marketing circles as a *buyer persona*. He initially drafted four personas and then narrowed it down to two that made the most sense for his business. He found that the role of his ideal client varied based on an organization's size. For large organizations, the ideal buyer was the person responsible for threat assessments. In other organizations, it was the person responsible for training.

Once he knew the type of individual to target, he dove deeper into what makes that person tick. He listed details like their organization size, industry, priorities, problems, and challenges. He added information on who they influence and how they are influenced.

Now, when ThreatSim creates a marketing message, they know exactly who they are writing it to and what their hot buttons are. Their buyer persona provides a detailed sketch of who they want to reach so they don't spin their wheels with people who are not their ideal targets.

Keep an Eye Out for Change

When Chris Schroeder, CEO of mobile application management firm App47, drafted his buyer personas for the first time, he included software developers. It made perfect sense at the time since the individuals within an enterprise who were tasked to develop a mobile app were the developers themselves. App47 is in a fast-changing industry, so Chris kept an eye out for how his ideal client profile might evolve. Within one year, he noticed that the actual buyers of his company's products and services were usually the senior executives or business owners rather than the developers. The developers still play a role - they influence the purchasing decision. But it's the senior executives and owners who have the budget authority to sign off on a project.

The personas Chris develops explore the specific pain points that an ideal customer has and matches it to a feature in App47's products. This exercise helps his team make the right pitch because they know what affects a buyer's thinking. And because of the speed with which mobile application development is moving, he revisits his buyer persona twice a year to be sure he is reaching the right client profile and can tweak his messaging appropriately.

Find Your Most Profitable Customers

Martijn van der Schaaf, CEO of Computication, was one of the first managed service providers in Holland to offer IT infrastructure and support for a fixed monthly price. Being first to market with a new business model gave him a competitive edge - for a while. At the time, he also offered web application development services, but soon retired that part of the business because he did not find it to be as scalable.

As competition crept in, Martijn realized he needed to re-evaluate his business. He enlisted the help of a market research consultant to create a survey for his existing clients. He wanted to know what type of client benefited most from his company's services, which ones were the easiest to sell to, and who was the most profitable.

Some of the questions he asked were:

- How did you hear about our company?

- Which factors influenced your decision process when you selected our company?

- Can you mention our 3 core values?

- Do you think our name is recognizable in the MSP market? If so, why? If not, why not?

- How do you think we can improve brand recognition?

- Who would you list as our 3 closest competitors?

The last question revealed some very interesting responses. He found that companies he thought were his competitors were not being mentioned by his customers. Some of his clients even struggled to name anyone.

Armed with insights from his financials and his new market research report, Martijn knew what he had to do next.

Instead of pursuing smaller companies that had 5 to 25 seats, he targeted companies with 100 or more seats. Instead of looking for all sorts of organizations, he narrowed his attention to four vertical markets. He revamped his marketing material to address the needs of this tightly focused group.

"The downside is that you have to say 'no' to some opportunities," says Martijn. His competitors offer a wide array of products and services to a wide range of customers. This spreads them thin. Martijn's focus on a particular persona empowers him to reach a specific type of client while lowering his overhead costs and simplifying his internal processes.

Not Just for Finding an Ideal Client

You can use the strategy of creating a buyer persona for more than just client profiles. ThreatSim creates personas for their public relations efforts, too. Once they know which blogs, magazines, and trade rags their target market reads, they look for writers who covered phishing attacks in the past. They are the ones most likely to write about this in the future.

TheatSim can send examples of how they have helped companies thwart attacks through employee training. By identifying the ideal writer's persona, they are providing laser-focused parameters for their team to reach the authors who are most likely to talk about their services.

What Goes Into Your Ideal Client Profile

To create a buyer persona for your company, take a look at your current customers to see who made the final purchasing decision. Chances are, it is not the person who was tasked with researching options for products or services like yours. Identify your ideal client using these parameters:

- Organization size

- Job title and role within the organization

- Key problems they face and how your solution saves them time and money, and relieves their headaches

- Roles of people who influence their decision process (subordinates like an internal IT department, advisers like lawyers or accountants)

- Budget and buying cycles

- Professional associations they join

- Conferences they attend

- Publications they read

Knowing when people make IT purchases will play a role in your strategy. Not everyone spends money on IT services consistently throughout the year. Federal government buyers spend more in the spring and even more in the summer due to their budget cycles. You should market to them heavily in the fall, just after their fiscal year starts, to get on their radar when their budget gets fully funded and they want to spend their allocation to avoid losing it.

State and local governments have different fiscal years, leading to different budgeting and buying cycles. It is important to take calendar-year timing into account in your persona so you know when to invest in various marketing tactics.

Your persona should also include how your ideal client gets information. The advantage of knowing what they read and where they hang out is that it tells you how to get in front of them. You will know what association networking events to attend and where to put your public relations efforts. You will increase your chances of meeting the right person to engage in a conversation.

Going through the exercise of profiling your buyer gives you the understanding of their buying process for selecting a technology vendor. If you target sophisticated buyers, such as CIOs or CTOs, your marketing collateral will require more technical depth than if you target people with less technical knowledge.

You can interview your existing clients to find out some of this information. Talk to your best ones, not the ones you wish you didn't have. Just ask them these basic who, what, why, and where questions:

- Who was involved in the decision process

- What factors were important to them in their evaluation

- Why they picked you over other companies

- Where they find out about or get recommendations for services like yours

Your personas will also help you identify the types of people you can reach through LinkedIn and other methods that I will talk about in future chapters.

Checklist: Your Next Steps

- Looking at your current customers, who makes the final purchasing decision? What is their job title and role within the organization?

- What key problems does this person face, and how could your solution save them time, money, and make their life easier?

- Who else influences their purchasing decision? What publications, conferences, or professional associations shape their views?

- How can you reach this person to share your solution?

- If you are having trouble creating your buyer persona, take some time to interview your best clients, asking them the questions above.

3

Honing Your Marketing Message

"Marketing is too important to be left to the marketing department." - David Packard

Knowing What to Say

O nce you know your ideal client profile, or your buyer persona, coming up with your marketing pitch becomes remarkably easier. Pretend your persona is a potential client. You can have a make-believe dialog with that person and imagine how they would respond. This will give you insight into preparing for real encounters with people who match your persona's characteristics.

An Elevator Speech that Leads to a Conversation

Could you convey the value of what you do in the time it takes an elevator to travel from the top floor of a building down to the lobby? If not, you need to develop and memorize your "elevator speech," which clearly and succinctly answers the question, "So, what do you do?"

Abraham Lincoln used to say that it would take him two weeks to write a 20-minute speech, but he could talk for two hours without any notice at all.

In business, you need a brief elevator speech as well as a detailed "follow-up." The brief version offers a nutshell view of your business, enough to whet the appetite of a potential customer and cause them to ask for more details. When they do, you are ready with your more detailed follow-up. Memorize both versions so you are never at a loss for explaining what you do.

The key to an effective elevator speech is to be specific. Consider this exercise: In 20 seconds or less, state clearly the kind of service you provide or the products you sell. Be specific.

I don't mean something like, "We do computer programming and system design." That hardly gives insight into what you do best. I also don't mean, "We develop software for database management, systems integration, network management, Windows applications, and other custom applications." Small businesses that do everything under the sun lose credibility.

Remember the deck contracting example from Chapter 1? Most people prefer to hire specialists. Specialists can typically charge far more than generalists. More so, you will find that when you specialize, you create an opportunity to be known for your specialty, a trait that can generate a lot of business.

A repairman that once came to my house to fix the refrigerator told me that he used to install and repair all types of appliances. But as time went on, he decided to focus on a certain brand of products. His business grew. Later he focused only on that brand's refrigerators. It turns out that there is a big market just for this in my metropolitan area. He is booked every day and has lowered his overhead expenses dramatically because he only needs to stock a limited number of parts. He also reduces his ongoing training time and costs to keep up to speed with new products.

Successful lawyers, accountants, real estate professionals, and consultants all carve out niches for their businesses. Sure, you've heard of large companies that provide an assortment of services. But that's just the point: those organizations are large. They've got entire departments devoted to getting customers. Small businesses must think and operate differently. By specializing, your size becomes one of your biggest advantages.

Here are some examples of elevator speeches, including both brief and detailed versions.

Example: Software Product

Brief version
My company provides a low-cost, email newsletter management tool for organizations to communicate with their customers and generate repeat business.

Follow-up details
We've found that companies who keep in touch with their customers regularly increase their chances of repeat business dramatically. Our tool makes this process easy. You can create and send professional-looking newsletters in just a few simple steps without having to learn any programming. We provide live, reports that detail how many people—and who—opened your

email message and clicked on the links within it. Our software runs over the Internet so there is nothing to download or install. Would you like to try it out for free?

Notice two key points:

1. The service's key benefit: making the process of getting repeat business easy.

2. The offer to try out the service for free at the end of the pitch.

Including a benefit highlights the value to a potential customer. Just saying what you do or sell isn't enough. Tell the listener what he or she can get out of using your service or product. Always try to close with some kind of offer whether it is a follow-up phone call, a free trial or consultation, or even something as simple as sending a copy of an article you found or wrote on the topic. Of course, not everyone you talk to will be able to use what you offer so look and listen for clues that suggest your words will get lost in the wind.

If you find yourself at a networking event talking to someone who is more focused on getting that next beer, stop wasting your time and mingle. The more people you can say your elevator speech to, the higher the chances of landing a new customer.

Example: Website Design Services

Brief version
My company helps people reach audiences online with smart design, straightforward navigation, and clear copywriting to educate their customers and effectively offer them their products, services, and expertise.

Follow-up details
While most web design companies focus on selling pricey graphics and other distracting design elements, our approach

focuses on identifying our customer's needs for information and problem-solving. We create websites that help our clients be the answer to questions their customers are asking online. We do this without unnecessary bells and whistles, and instead, create a useful, relevant, visible website for our clients. What do you hope your customers do when they first visit your website? What do you think they actually do?

In this example, the question requesting a call to action at the end is not something like "Are you satisfied with your website?" or "Would you be open to a free consultation to explore options to manage your website better?" Instead, it is an open-ended question designed to engage the listener in a dialog. This gives you a chance to probe for areas in which you can find an opening to request a meeting, if appropriate.

Your Turn

Now it's your turn. Take a moment. Think hard. Write it down. Edit it. Write something else. Check it. Test it out on a partner, colleague, or even your significant other.

After you write your own brief version, memorize it. Try to memorize as much of your detailed version as possible, too. If you haven't taken the time to write it down, stop reading! Don't continue until you have written a concise description of the services or products you provide.

With this statement committed to memory, you will be able to tell people what you do clearly, without stumbling -- and in the time it takes the elevator to reach the lobby.

Connecting with Your Potential Clients' Hot Buttons

Having your elevator speech is important. It has to be used appropriately. Talking about yourself too much when you meet someone new is not a good idea. It can be a turn off and you could lose their attention forever.

The skill of knowing what to say and when to say is not hard to develop. I've found these three steps to work well:

1. Overcome the desire to talk about yourself.

2. Get others to talk about themselves.

3. Listen for the types of comments they are making. It will tell you what stage of the buying process they are in.

Every buyer goes through three different stages in their buying cycle:

- Awareness of the problem

- Research to find options for solutions

- Decision on which solution to use

Similarly, you have three stages of buyers:

- Prospect

- Lead

- Opportunity

At each stage, a potential buyer of your services has different questions. Ask yourself what those questions are and what business needs the person is trying to address at that stage of awareness. The value of exploring the thought process of each stage is that it allows you to be prepared with a set of appropriate responses. Instead of jumping into a sales pitch designed to close a deal, you would be able to filter out that a person isn't mentally ready to make a commitment yet and your line of questions can help guide them down the path to your solution. Your questions will be different for each persona.

For example, Ed Mana of Technology on Demand, who targets his managed services to audio-visual companies, might find that his buyer persona would ask the following questions:

Prospect stage

- How do I manage my email and office documents?

- How can I manage my billing more efficiently?

- How can I track all of my assets?

- Who in my organization would be responsible for managing this?

Lead stage

- How do I make sure that I don't lose my data in the event of a natural disaster?

- How do I keep my data secure?

- Should I hire a person to do this in-house or outsource it to another company?

- What's all this talk about "cloud" stuff?

- What skills do I need to look for in a person or company that could do this?

- What should I expect to see in a service level agreement (SLA)?

Opportunity stage

- Which companies provide these services?

- What exactly will they do? What are the deliverables?

- What is my role? My company's role?

- What is the investment? The return on investment?

- What are the contract terms? The response time and SLA?

These questions will help you hone the different messages that would interest a buyer.

Sales Messaging vs. Educational Messaging

As you read this book, you will notice an emphasis on educating prospects and how education is very different from selling.

Sales messaging includes the traditional marketing language of features, benefits, and pricing. This type of messaging can turn off a prospect if he feels threatened, doesn't understand the value of what you are offering, or simply isn't ready to make a purchase just yet.

Educational messaging, on the other hand, teaches your prospect how to do something better. If you offer search engine optimization (SEO) services, you can teach prospects how to find the best keywords for their industry. If you sell accounting software, you can educate prospects on compliance issues.

Sales messaging says, "Buy my products or services because I am the best."

Educational messaging says, "Let me show you how to solve your business problems."

The focus is on the prospect and giving them the resources he needs to run their business better. This type of messaging positions you as an informed, trusted source. It encourages your prospects to turn to you for advice and, when the time is right, your products and services.

If you are unsure about whether your messaging falls into sales territory, imagine that your message is an article to be published in a magazine. Ask yourself which section your article would appear under. Would it be under company news, industry trends, or best practices?

If it is company news, then your article is a sales piece. I'm not saying that there is anything wrong with this -- there is a time and place for sales messaging. Just be clear on what type it is because you will use each one differently.

Let's consider the questions posed by the buyer persona, presented in the stages I outlined above. As people move through the buying stages, from the prospect stage to the lead stage to the opportunity stage, your messaging will go from educational to sales.

For example, during the prospect stage, people are seeking information. If you can be the one to provide it, you will establish trust and nurture them along to the next stage.

Using the sample question, "How do I manage my email and office documents?" you can produce an article to educate the person on that very subject. It could be called, "How to Effectively Manage Email and Documents in the Office."

After reading this article, the prospect may be qualified to become a lead because you have piqued his interest by showing how his problem could be solved.

In the lead stage, you are still educating, but you'll want to start nudging the lead towards your services. For the sample question, "How do I make sure that I don't lose my data in the event of a natural disaster?" you could produce an article called, "Checklist for Keeping Your Data Safe During a Natural Disaster."

Now, you are teaching the lead about preparing his data for a natural disaster, but you should also let him know there are specific services available that are designed to assist him every step of the way.

At this point, the lead trusts you even more, and now he is looking for a service to help him with his needs. He has moved into the opportunity stage.

When the lead asks, "Which companies provide these services?" you might hand him a white paper that provides information to consider as he looks for a solution provider. It could include a checklist for what to look for in a provider, what the provider should offer, and what the lead's role will be in the process. At the end of the white paper, you have included your company's contact information so that the lead can get in touch. Again, you have educated the lead, but you are also nudging him further along towards buying.

When you follow up, you can really start focusing on your sales messaging because you have laid the foundation for it. Your lead is open to what you have to say because he sees you as knowledgeable, as someone who cares about his business's success, and as a trusted ally.

As you can see, there are times when educational messaging is beneficial, but there are also times when sales messaging works best. Educational messaging should start early on in your sales process - and continue even after you have acquired the client. Sales messaging should be reserved for the latter buying stages when you have established a position of trust and knowledge.

Checklist: Your Next Steps

- Take some time to review your company's messaging. Does it fall into the educational or the sales category? Get very clear on when you should use each type of messaging so you do not accidentally start a sales pitch when you should be asking more probing questions.

- What are your ideal client's needs at the Prospect Stage of the buying process? How can you provide them with the information they are seeking right now?

- What are your ideal client's needs at the Lead Stage of the buying process? How can you provide them with the resources they need now?

- What does your ideal client need at the Opportunity Stage of the buying process? How can you provide the information they need to make a buying decision now?

- Using the examples above as guidelines to write your own elevator speech, including the brief version, and the follow-up details. Edit and refine your speech. Now, practice it until you have it memorized.

4

Pricing Strategies That Make it Easier for Clients to Buy

"Price is what you pay. Value is what you get." - Warren Buffett

O f all the four P's in marketing, pricing may be the most oversimplified and, therefore, most misunderstood. (The other P's of marketing are product, promotion, and place.) Pricing a product or service isn't just about covering your costs while staying competitive within your market - while hopefully turning a profit. The price you set can have a tremendous impact on whether customers decide to buy your products and services at all.

Your pricing strategy should aim for one major goal: to make it easy for people to digest exactly what it is they are buying from you. Early on, I learned that if you price IT services at an hourly rate, it's hard for clients to know what they are getting. These clients may know what they want, but they may not understand how many hours it will take, what their end product will necessarily be, or what the total cost of these services are.

Pricing By Value, Not By Time

A computer expert is asked to visit a company to diagnose a problem and fix a computer. He looks at the computer for a few minutes, and quickly realizes what the problem is. So, he pushes a button on the machine, and the problem is fixed.

The computer expert gives the client an invoice for $500. But, the client is perplexed and wants to know why the invoice is so high, considering that the computer expert only worked for a very short amount of time. He gives the invoice back to the computer expert to fix it.

So, the computer expert outlines the work on the invoice in the following way:

Pushing the button = $5.00
Knowing which button to push = $495.00

Itemizing your bill this way might cause you to lose some clients. It does not explain the value of what they are getting, only the price. Clients who buy only on price are not your best customers. They will continue to shop around for something cheaper.

Does this scenario sound familiar? Are your clients perplexed when the bill comes because, while they understand the value of the services you provide, they can't grasp the way you've assigned a price to this value?

This problem inevitably results from the mindset that quality work requires a prerequisite amount of time to complete. Your pricing strategy should be to charge for the *value* of what you are delivering to someone, not necessarily how much time it's going to take.

Packaging Your Service as a Product

One way IT service companies can clarify the value they offer clients is to package their services as a product and then create a menu of options to make it easier for a prospect to understand what they are getting.

This approach benefits clients and companies alike. It gives your business the opportunity to create a proposal, outlining the scope of the work you will perform and the estimated cost, and then to post it on your website for prospects to see.

Let's say you provide Hosted Exchange services. Your menu would list all the benefits -- not just features -- that clients will get from your services, along with pricing. Aim to structure the menu so that people can look at your services as a bundled package, and even select the services they need a la carte. Your pricing sheet would include each feature and benefit that is included with each bundle. If it makes sense for your business, include the a la carte pricing to show the savings if the customer buys the bundled package. Packages enable people to get a clearer picture of what they are buying from you.

Consider the way wireless communication companies price their services. They offer their services packaged in all sorts of ways. Customers can purchase cell phone service based on how much data they use, or they can buy an unlimited data plan. Cable companies offer tiers of service that include Internet, television and phone service.

Similarly, IT companies can price services on their website in different packages -- from a bundled pre-priced package to a la carte services -- so people can clearly see their choices and select what works best for them.

The Assessment Product

A smart way to package your services is to create an assessment product. To entice prospects to try your services, you can create an audit product for a specified price. When a client purchases your audit product, you will assess their company and provide a complete evaluation, giving them an unbiased view on whatever it is that you do (disaster recovery audit, SEO audit, etc.). Then, you can offer them a checklist of what they should do to improve in your area of expertise.

You may want to offer this assessment product as a freebie if it doesn't take much time and will get you more work. If you can quickly go in and show the client where the bottlenecks are, your assessment product may lead to a substantial amount of additional, paid work.

Another way to entice prospects with a bundled package is to offer an introductory product that can lead to future, more in-depth work. For example, let's say that a web design firm wants to offer a "Quick-Start Package," which consists of a basic, five-page website including 10 stock images, an About Us page, and the structure to enable the client to build out a solid, starter website.

Once a client is willing to purchase this starter package from you, she may be more open to hiring you for more high-level work down the road, such as developing web applications or creating software products. But to win these future purchases, which require a longer time commitment and can't easily be packaged, you'll need to showcase your expertise. So, stick to the more basic services you can offer clients as a loss leader incentive and then aim to win bigger projects from them as you build trust.

It's up to you whether or not you use this assessment product as a loss leader, in other words, as something you give away for free to get more business later. You may want to charge a small fee if the assessment will take more of your time than you're willing to give away for free. Whatever you decide, be sure to test it to make sure it is ultimately generating more business. After all, all effective pricing strategies should lead to one place -- increased revenue for your company.

Using a Loss Leader to Get More Consulting Business

Retail companies use a "loss leader" all of the time to get more business. You've probably seen sales for $1 or even $0.01 products that are clearly priced below their cost. Retailers use this strategy to get you in the store in the hopes that you will buy much more than the loss leader product. Usually those loss leaders are scattered throughout the store so that you see many other products that you might want to buy along the way. It usually works. Websites place loss leaders near related high-margin products to encourage more sales (and typically charge for shipping to discourage people who only want the loss leader at the heavily discounted price).

You can also use a loss leader for a consulting business, but in a different way. Since your "product" is consulting services, offering yourself for a $1 rate would sound ridiculous to a client and would devalue what you bring to the table. Never discount yourself like that! Instead, you can offer to do a small project for free. This would be something that takes you an hour or two, or a little more if you are comfortable with that.

Offering an initial consultation like this does two things:

1. Gives the client a taste of the value you will bring to their organization.

2. Gives you an opportunity to see what working with this client is really like.

Free High-Value Consulting Session

I had a client who was almost ready to engage, but was slow in pulling the trigger. During our conversations, I asked several questions that uncovered a laundry list of ways I could help. They seemed excited, but they were hesitating to get started. As I probed to find out why, I figured out they were looking at the price, not the value. So, I picked one of their most pressing topics as my loss leader and offered a free one-hour in-depth consulting session about it.

During our conversation, I didn't keep track of time and we did run over an hour. I also did not sell my services during this free consultation because I wanted them to experience what it would be like to actually work with me. I only focused on their problem and asked probing questions that got deeper into the real issues (see Chapter 6 for a list of questions). I was able to offer several on-point solutions that provided a direct benefit very quickly. They were able to see that I had their best interest at heart.

When they compared the value they received to the price of my rates, it was clear that they were getting a good deal. They made back more than they invested. After that dialog, they were ready to ask more questions about other issues they were facing. When you provide rock solid consulting services, people see the value.

You can also offer a free half- or one-day training seminar at a customer's site to educate them on a particular topic. If a prospect is looking to implement a workflow solution, a morning seminar on the pain points, the options and the expected results is a great way to show off your expertise.

Responding to Pushback

To ward off attempts to gain more of my consulting insight for free, I asked if they would like to tackle some of their other issues as well under a more formal agreement between our companies. That helped them understand that I wasn't prepared to give more away for free. You can use responses like these if a prospect keeps trying to get your advice for free:

> *I appreciate your question and it is definitely something I can help with. Shall we go ahead with our formal agreement so that we can get started right away?*

> *This question warrants a deeper discussion and I want to make sure that the time that both of us invest in solving these issues is spent efficiently. There's no 5 or 10 minute solution to this topic so rather than start a dialog that we can't finish, how about we move forward with an engagement letter? This way, I can make sure you're on my calendar and that I can give the topic the full attention it deserves.*

> *I hope the value you gained from our prior consultation illustrated how we can help go deep into solving problems. So rather than start a conversation that only touches the surface, let's proceed with moving forward in a more formal way. Shall I send you our engagement letter?*

If you encounter a company that isn't ready to engage you even after your initial consultation and after trying the responses above, watch for signs that they do not have the budget to hire you. The worst situation you can be in is engaging a consulting client that can't pay you.

When Not to Use a Loss Leader

Not all consulting services lend themselves to a loss leader consultation in which you can provide in-depth advice. Often, consulting requires deeper, long-term commitments. In these cases, your initial consultations need to focus on problem discovery so your proposal addresses the client's key questions and not something that you think they want.

For those times when you need to nudge a prospect to close a deal, give them a taste - just a morsel - of what you can do for free. Don't discount your services because then your value will be the discount, not your knowledge.

Positioning Yourself for Outsourcing

Another consideration in your pricing strategy should be the reason businesses choose to outsource in the first place. Position your IT services so that businesses wanting to outsource will choose you.

Consider the following example: When it comes to having a meal prepared for you, you can either hire a personal chef or go eat at a restaurant. In this example, hiring a personal chef is the in-house solution (hiring someone in-house to do the work you don't have time for), and eating at a restaurant is the outsourced solution.

While both scenarios involve having someone prepare your meal, you will have to pay the personal chef annually or per hour to retain his services. Sure, there will be a predictable fixed cost and you can guarantee having access to this food, but retaining a personal chef can get really expensive.

Maybe you don't need professionally prepared food for every meal you eat; perhaps you only want a meal like that for special occasions or for the summer when lots of friends and family come to visit. If that is the case, it will be more cost-effective for you to eat at a restaurant only when you want those special meals -- in other words, to outsource.

Another reason to choose the restaurant is that, while your professional chef may make the best Thai cuisine you've ever had, sometimes you just might be in the mood for Italian. With IT services, an in-house IT team probably has expertise in many areas, but it's nearly impossible for them to be good at everything. So, from time to time, businesses will look to outsourcing to fill in the gaps in their own IT departments. In this case, you want to position yourself so that businesses will come to you for the outside expertise they need.

Let's look at another IT services example. Web design companies are often hired by businesses that have some basic knowledge of creating a website. Sure, they can develop a bare-bones website in-house. But, what if they want to do things that require web development skills beyond the basics, like creating a custom web application?

In this situation, a web design company should pitch their services to the client as an enhancement of the current in-house capabilities. This company should position itself as having the expertise to take that basic website to the next level with a more comprehensive deliverable, by providing access to its high-end graphic designers, app programmers, and web architects.

Checklist: Your Next Steps

- Consider the services that you offer. Is the value you provide to your clients easy to see? Do you need to adjust your pricing strategy to help potential clients understand what you can do for their business?

- Could you package your services as a product, such as a bundle of services to be purchased as a single product? Create a pricing sheet outlining the features and benefits of each item included in the bundle.

- Do you offer a service that businesses would like to outsource? Create a pitch to prospects that offers your services as an enhancement to what they already have in-house. Consider the expertise you could provide that they may be lacking.

- Could you offer an assessment product as a free or low-cost package to let prospects try out your services? What would you include in the assessment that would provide the prospect with value without consuming too much of your time and resources?

- Would offering the assessment product as a loss leader pave the way for future, high-end projects with your prospects?

- Have you considered offering a free, high-value consulting session? What would you offer? How long would it last? How would you respond to push back?

PART 2

GET SET

5

The #1 Way to Work Your Referral Network

"In sales, a referral is the key to the door of resistance." - Bo Bennett

Ring... ring... ring... "Hi, this is John. I'm not in right now. Please leave a message." Sound familiar? If you don't know John, he probably won't return your call - or your email. You can change this scenario. In this chapter, I will share the best way to make that connection happen, as well as what to do to keep your network growing and producing new business.

What Every Business Owner Wants

There are five valuable things you can offer a prospect to encourage them to reach back and connect with you. They involve putting money in their pocket, keeping money in their pocket and helping them sleep better at night.

1. A Live Lead: This one works like magic. It is by far the #1 way to get someone to return your call or reply to your email. Every business owner wants a qualified lead that helps them make more money. Providing the gift of a live lead will make a lasting impression and start a dialog where none existed before.

Where do you find leads to share? It's a lot easier than you might think. Here's how:

Suppose you come across someone who is looking to hire a graphic designer. Maybe you saw a posting on LinkedIn or someone mentioned it at a networking event. If you are a managed services provider, then graphic design might not be in your roster of services. But, someone in your network or extended network might know just the right person to fit the bill.

So, instead of letting that casual comment about someone else's need fall by the wayside, you can use the opportunity to reach out to someone you would like to connect with. Can anyone in your circles in LinkedIn, Facebook, professional groups, or your client or prospect base provide graphic design services? Finding someone in your prospect base is ideal because it creates a unique opportunity for everyone involved.

Once you identify several companies that might be interested in the opportunity, reach out with an email. The subject line should simply say, "Can you help with this lead for graphic design services?"

Your email can read like this:

> Bob, I just came across a business lead and I thought of you. A colleague of mine is looking for graphic design services for his new website. If this might be a fit for your business, please let me know and I'll connect you. If not, no worries... I'm happy to send along other leads as I come across them.

Next, send an email to the person in search of graphic design services. It could say this:

> Jody, I know of a couple of companies who might be able to help you with your graphic design requirement. Let me know if you'd like me to connect you.

What usually happens next is pretty amazing. If you send this lead to a prospect, they are extremely likely to reach out. In other words, that prospect who you've been trying to get in touch with for months will likely be contacting you.

The key is not to give away all the lead's information in your email. Your goal is to get that person to reach back to you so that you can establish a personal connection. This method works because you are giving someone business, or trying to solve an issue they are facing. These things show everyone you connect with that you are looking out for their interests, even if the opportunity doesn't work out.

This also affords you the perfect opportunity to create a dialog with your prospect and work the product or service that *you* sell into the conversation.

So, if you're having trouble reaching out to someone because they aren't returning your phone calls, find a lead to send them. It's a very successful tactic that gets attention quickly. You can find opportunities to share everywhere; you just have to keep your eyes peeled and your ears open. Whenever you hear about a need that you can't fulfill, find someone who can and make the connections.

2. A Way to Make More Money: The second thing you can offer a prospect is connected to the first because, once again, it positions you as someone who can help. If you offer a tool or service that can help someone make more money, you can be there to scratch that itch they haven't been able to reach.

Companies and nonprofits alike want to make more money. Get them to see how you can help them by showing a direct correlation between what you offer and how it will increase revenue for their organization. In your pitch, be sure to include concrete examples of how other companies have gotten results from your product or service.

3. A Way to Cut Costs: Bringing in more revenue isn't the only way you can help a company increase their bottom line. Maybe your products and services can help a company decrease their costs, too.

Suppose you are an IT firm that is targeting a healthcare provider. You want to take over the provider's claims processing by offering a way to automate their current paper system. To sell this healthcare provider your services, you'll need to demonstrate how your electronic solution will cut the cost of managing records.

In this particular situation, you may also need to create fear in their minds about bad things that can happen and then show how your company can alleviate that fear. For example, what if the healthcare provider experiences a disaster and loses all of its data? Or, what if it runs into a problem complying with HIPAA regulations? Show them how your services can help backup their data for safekeeping, as well as how you can help keep them organized to meet their reporting needs -- all while saving money with your more efficient system.

4. A Way to Save Time and Increase Productivity: Can you offer a prospect a way to be more efficient? Paint a picture of how your product or service will help a business reduce time for tasks that your prospect currently does or how your technology can help reduce bottlenecks and improve processes. If you can provide an executive with ways they can be more efficient in their work, they will undoubtedly value your relationship and seek out a conversation with you.

5. A Way to Achieve Peace of Mind: Insurance companies build their businesses on this very principle. All companies want to feel more secure, so if you are selling data backup and recovery services, what you are really selling is peace of mind. In other words, you are trying to ease the FUD Factor of *f*ear, *u*ncertainty, and *d*oubt within your prospects. Let these companies know that you can take their worries away, or at least help them to mitigate their risks.

Networking in a Nutshell: Be the Connector

Cultivating a rich network that provides new business takes time and effort. Your energy is best spent on targeted efforts that have a deliberate outcome.

What do you do when you meet someone who is looking to get advice or to have work done? Just being the connection between two people can position you as the person who can help others find resources.

Where to Meet Prospects
Join organizations that your customers belong to. Don't just join associations filled with the same types of companies as yours.

Remember Ed Mana of Technology On Demand, who I introduced to you in Chapter 1? Since Ed is an MSP, he is likely already involved in a professional organization or two that focuses on the types of technology services he provides. But, his target market is not at the networking events Ed attends.

Ed's best bet for prospecting is to join an audio-visual association in his local area. Attending those meetings would place him directly in front of a pool of targeted prospects. If a couple of these prospects become clients, Ed can easily expand his reach since these business owners are likely to talk to each other. Just by getting involved in a wider association network, Ed could become the MSP provider of choice in his niche.

What to Do

It is not enough just to join a bunch of associations - you need to be active to get the most bang for your membership buck. I only join an association if I know that I will become an active member in the very first year, and I will get on the board within the first few years.

Once you become an officer or board member, the connections really start to happen. Other members come to you to find ways to get involved, etc., and you become a hub and will meet many more people than if you were the type of member who just occasionally shows up for meetings.

If all you do is attend meetings, you are selling yourself short and missing out on ready-made opportunities to expand your marketing to a broader base of prospects.

What to Say

Once you have the opportunity to speak with a prospect, what you say isn't as important as what you don't say. Don't start pitching your services or just talking about yourself. Get them to talk about themselves by asking questions and focusing on what they have to say.

When I meet new people, I like to ask the following question:

> *What kind of issues are you facing right now as you grow your business?*

This question sets the stage for people to share their business needs. Don't ask this superficially. If you really aren't interested, they will notice because you will likely appear distracted when they answer. I ask questions like this genuinely all the time. Putting an emphasis on helping the people you meet creates goodwill. If I find that they are looking for help in a particular area, I think about who in my network I can connect them to for follow up.

Most people enjoy talking about themselves and their issues, so when you ask this question and are honestly interest, they are likely to open up to you. It doesn't matter what your background is or your specialty.

When you listen carefully, you can spot opportunities to help people solve their problems. You can work your 30-second elevator pitch into the conversation if you feel you may be able to help them solve a problem by leveraging your network.

How to Follow Up

After you have made a connection and exchanged business cards at a networking event, don't let that connection wither away. First, add your new contacts to your email list and to your LinkedIn account.

Next, make yourself stand out from the pack by doing this one simple thing. I have personalized, folded note cards that have my name on the front. The inside of the card is blank. When I meet someone to whom I'd like to extend an extra "nice to meet you" or "thank you," whether they've given me a referral or invited me to a nice business event, I use these cards to send a quick note. I say something short like this:

> Mike, it was great seeing you at the business social last week. Let's keep in touch.

When I mail a handwritten note like this, people tend to remember me because so few take the time and care to personalize a connection in this way.

Another way to use the handwritten note is to personally thank a speaker for his or her contribution and insight at an event you attended. Imagine that you are waiting in a line of about 25 people to shake hands and exchange business cards with a speaker at a networking event. By the time you get to the front of that line, you can bet the speaker won't be able to remember you from the next guy.

Use the note card method to reach out and personally thank the speaker for his presentation. Include your business card, and mail it out the next day. Add this sentence to your note: "Look for my LinkedIn connection request online." There's a very good chance that the speaker will remember you.

Speaking of business cards, be sure to include your vCard in all follow up email messages, too. That way, the recipient has all your contact information immediately and you can become part of their contact list with a simple click.

When you supplement your in-person and electronic communication with the type of personal connection I discussed above, you are reinforcing any connections you make. It may not work with everyone, but it will make a memorable impression on those who are interested in networking as well.

There are lots of books about how to work a room and how to get people to share information about themselves. *How to Win Friends and Influence People* by Dale Carnegie is a classic if you want to develop your skills further.

Offer an Incentive

Paul Tomlinson, CEO of Mirus IT Solutions in England, encourages happy customers to talk about his company and send him more business. To get feedback, he sends automated customer satisfaction emails to his clients through a professional services automation tool.

When someone rates his company's service very highly, he sends another automated email asking for a referral. He offers an incentive. Anyone who refers a prospect to Mirus is entered into a monthly drawing for a two-night stay at a local spa and is given a bottle of champagne - regardless of whether the referral turns into a customer or not. The bottle is delivered personally by the client's account manager to reinforce the personal touch.

Imagine the warm feeling you would give your clients if you brought a bottle of champagne as an expression of gratitude on your next appointment. The client might not remember what you talk about that day, but they will always remember the kind gesture. They may also be motivated to send you more referrals.

Although Paul employs many different techniques to generate leads, referrals account for 50% of all new business. He gets about four new qualified leads from referrals each month and converts them into customers 90% of the time.

Tying It All Together

Here's a summary of what I have found to be the top tips for networking:

1. Get actively and visibly involved in associations you belong to. Seek out ones that extend into your clients' industry focus so you get in front of others like your current client base - those are the people who could buy your services.

2. When you meet people, get them to talk about themselves - be careful not to spend most of your interaction doing the talking yourself. Ask them what issues they are currently facing in their business, and think of people in your network who could help them

if the issues fall outside your area of expertise.

3. Once you have made a connection, follow up to be sure you are remembered.

4. Most importantly, be a connector. Seek out and share leads so you can be that connector between someone who has a specific business need and a prospect who can fulfill that need - and with whom you can nurture your own business relationship.

5. Say thanks when you get a referral. Whether you send a handwritten note or a bottle of champagne, acknowledge the person who thought of you, even if their referral did not turn into new business.

Checklist: Your Next Steps

- Start leveraging your LinkedIn network, as well as your in-person network, to help people find what they're looking for, including: a live lead, a way to make more money, a way to cut costs, a way to save time and increase productivity, and a way to achieve peace of mind. Make a point to scan LinkedIn and other social networks for both business needs and people who could fulfill those needs, on a regular basis.

- Look for organizations outside your regular network or industry. Are there any you could join that would connect you with new prospects?

- Make a plan to become active in any organizations you join. Can you work towards becoming a board member or getting involved on a committee within the organization?

- Practice your networking skills, and remember to ask open-ended questions that get people talking about their business needs and the problems they are currently facing. Could your listening skills need some fine-tuning?

- Develop your own system for following up with people you meet at networking events. Besides exchanging business cards, would you benefit from sending a vCard or even a handwritten note?

- Embrace your new role as a connector; seek out and share leads, and leverage your connections to help people you would like to do business with.

6

Questions That Uncover Hidden Sales Opportunities

"Successful people ask better questions and, as a result, they get better answers." - Tony Robbins

The Hidden Sales Rep

You don't want to see your valuable client choosing another company for telecommunications services because they thought you only provided Hosted Exchange and nothing else. If you go to them after they've selected another vendor, you'll hear unfortunate comments like "Oh, I didn't know you guys did that. Sorry, we've already signed a 2-year contract with this other company."

Not only would that be a shock to your gut - and wallet, you've now let another cat in the house. That's bad news that could have been avoided. You have competition because that telecom company probably also offers managed services and is itching to get a piece of your action.

Existing clients are the lowest bar for getting more business. Without a sales person constantly probing for needs, these hidden sales opportunities are often lost.

Don't worry. There is a way to avoid this situation. You already have a hidden inside sales team.

Your Lowest Hanging Fruit

Most technical people don't like to sell. Some go as far as seeing sales and marketing as an activity on the dark side, something they would never see themselves doing. Yet sales are critical to business success.

The easiest way to get more sales is to offer additional options to existing customers. These are people who already put their faith in you for many of their technology needs. They don't see your sales reps anymore because they have already been sold.

Small technology service firms may not have individual account reps to be the liaison between your clients and your technical staff. That means the people closest to your existing customers are your technical team members - the engineers, technicians, and customer support reps who interact with your clients daily. They are the problem-solvers that your clients have grown to rely on and trust.

Trust enables a lot of things to happen. When clients trust your technology recommendations and solutions, you become part of their inner circle of advisers. Your team's suggestions mean a lot because without them, your client would have to find another reliable source for technology, or suffer the consequences of bad technical judgment calls. You are as important as their lawyer or accountant because they know you have their best interest in mind.

Questions That Uncover Untapped Opportunities

If you can get your technical team to ask certain questions to clients on a regular basis, you can uncover opportunities waiting to be tapped. The key is to engage your clients in an open-ended dialog about their business, not just their technology issues.

While you may be there just to support technical work, they have a broader view. They are dealing with many other problems that need solving. Try to see the world through your client's eyes. Once you have established trust, you can inquire about their business plans and goals, the obstacles they are trying to overcome, and their wish list for an ideal world.

Your technical team may not have a business background, but they can be trained to ask leading questions that start a conversation about a client's high-level needs. When they share this newly found data with your team at staff meetings, you may spot trends across multiple clients and opportunities for adding a new product line or service. You will also gain insight into ways to position your company to make these new sales.

Here are questions that your technical team can ask to start a conversation that can lead to more sales. By asking these questions, you also demonstrate that you care for your client's business, which leads to a stronger bond of trust.

Some of the questions you could ask might focus on uncovering problems or issues the prospect wants to fix. Examples of these types of questions include:

- What kinds of things go wrong in your daily operations? Are any of these things that you would like to change?

- Assuming that you weren't limited by technology or financial resources, what would you change right now in your business processes?

- What could you or would you do if you had more time in the work day?

- If you could automate one thing about your job, what would it be?

When Andy Rudin was a salesperson for a large services company, he learned the hard way just how important it is to ask the right questions. Andy was meeting with a prospect who was a large multinational company that ships its products all over the world.

He asked them what kinds of things go wrong in their daily operations. He found out that sometimes people put the wrong load on a truck, so a shipment meant for Memphis ends up in Minneapolis instead.

Andy felt he had hit on a major pain point for the company, so he went back to his office and wrote a proposal worth several hundred thousand dollars to help solve this client's problem. This was a tiny fraction of this company's operations and Andy's company could save them significantly more than the investment.

The client declined.

Why? As Andy analyzed what happened, he discovered that there was one big question left unanswered: "Does it matter if the wrong products are shipped?"

It turned out that receiving the wrong products really wasn't that big of a deal for this company. The stores would simply put the products on their shelves and sell them anyway.

Andy now runs Outside Technologies, which provides sales strategy consulting services, and wrote about the experience. He said that he didn't know this important detail because he didn't ask that key follow-up question after probing for a need:

- Does it matter if...?

Another area to question prospects and clients about is their projected growth, which can help you uncover opportunities to assist them in scaling to meet this growth. Here are some examples:

- What kind of growth are you expecting in the next 12 months?

- How many new employees do you expect to add next year?

- Are you looking to add new products or services to your business? Tell me about it.

- Have you thought about what kind of infrastructure changes you might need to support this growth?

Suppose you ask a client one of these questions and he tells you his company is looking to add 25 new employees in the coming year.

Your response to his statement should be follow-up questions:

- Have you thought about the infrastructure details like how you will handle the additional employees' email, data, and remote access?

Now, you've started a dialog that can uncover opportunities to help solve these new issues your client is facing.

I was talking to a client who provides unified communications services across devices like laptops, tablets, and phones. Some of his clients may not even know technology like this exists, and they would be happy to know they could access all of these services through one interface. In this case, my client could serve as an educator to let his own clients know what technical capabilities are available to make their lives easier.

You should always tailor your questions based both on your industry and the industry of your clients. For example, if you sell disaster recovery solutions, there are plenty of ways to get prospects and clients thinking about the potential gaps in their continuity plan. For example, you could ask:

- If we had a storm that knocked out power at the office for several days like we did earlier this year, what kind of remote work plan do you have in place?

- If a hurricane like Katrina or Sandy happened here, how would you contact your staff? Your customers? What would happen to your files? Your business?

- Would you like some suggestions on how to devise a remote work plan, including the things you'll need to have in place to make it happen?

In the disaster recovery industry, you may be able to gather some clues before planning your pitch. For example, does your prospect's office look like it's in need of disaster recovery itself?

If your prospect's office is disheveled, with papers everywhere and organization nowhere to be found, you may not have a good chance of closing the deal. After all, if the prospect doesn't place a high priority on organization in general, he may not be organized about disaster planning either.

On the other hand, if the prospect has a tidy office, with everything in its place, then it's a good bet that he likes to know where all of his files are. Since he values organization, you have a better chance of selling disaster recovery and data backup services to him.

Sometimes people just do things a certain way because that is the way it's always been done. They may not think that a technology solution could make their processes more streamlined, or they may not even know what is available to them.

In this case, you can probe for areas where your technology services could improve their business and educate them on the tech solutions available on the market today. You might ask:

- How do you handle network security for your teleworkers?

- What would happen to your data, network access and website if a staff member lost a company laptop at an airport?

After asking these questions, you may have a story to share about a client whose data was hacked or lost. This will get them thinking about how such a security breach could affect their business, too.

If you are a website services provider, you may want to ask:

- What terms do your clients say they type into Google to find products or services like yours?

- If you were a prospect for your own services and did a search on Google, what words in the search results page would prompt you to click?

- If a customer's first interaction with you was your website, what would you hope they would do? What do you really think they would do?

These questions are useful because they force the prospect to look at his website from his customers' point of view. This honest assessment will open him up to your suggestions for improvement, such as adding resources to help website owners serve their customers better.

This conversation could then segue into a dialog about mobile support. You could ask:

- What are some of the recent mobile support options you have explored?

If you happen to sell and install hardware, you can also position your products and services as ways to make your prospects' lives easier. Some questions to ask include:

- How old are your oldest servers? Printers?

- Did you know that you can integrate your telecommunications and office network together so you get an email that reads a voicemail message to you?

- Do you ever find yourself wanting to do more work on your iPad but run into limitations and have to get your laptop?

These types of questions can also guide you in your pitch because they allow you to gauge where the prospect is in the buying cycle. For example, if they tend to hold on to computers for four to five years, then you might not have much of a chance to sell new technology often. If, however, they replace computers every two to three years, you can make a calendar note to get in touch with that prospect about six months or a year ahead of their next scheduled upgrade.

Speaking of upgrades, some prospects are hesitant to upgrade their software because they don't understand the value new features could provide, or because they are simply afraid of the unknown.

In this situation, I find that an effective way to frame the dialog is to ask this question:

- Have you explored the business case for upgrading to the latest version of (whatever software you sell)?

When you pose this question, you aren't selling; you are getting the prospect to ponder what it would mean to upgrade and what benefits an upgrade could provide.

Other questions to ask to gently get prospects thinking about upgrades include:

- What software that you currently use causes you the most headaches?

- How long does your staff take to <name whatever you can help with: do invoicing, organize resumes, coordinate logistics, etc.>?

- I know you've got SharePoint installed. What other ways does your staff collaborate?

After you have a lot of background on their problem, suggest your ideas as a question, like this:

- If you had a way to make sure you never lost your data and knew that it was secure no matter what mother nature did, would that something worth pursuing?

Get acknowledgement before you run back to the office and write a proposal. You need to know if you've hit upon a real concern or something that would be nice to have. The "nice to have" projects don't get funded.

Pitching Mr. Know-It-All

Sometimes, you will encounter Mr. Know-It-All. No matter what you ask, he will say he already has it solved. You can tell you are dealing with a "know it all" by his demeanor, often arrogant and sometimes even belligerent - you can see his colleagues reluctant to go to battle with him. His subordinates stay quiet for fear of being ridiculed.

In the early days of the Internet when I was building my first company, GovCon, a business development portal for government contractors, I was asked to present some technical options to the CEO of a 1,000-person firm. He brought my company in because we had a very strong reputation for helping government contractors like his. He had the reputation of being tough as nails and I wasn't looking forward to the meeting.

As we started the dialog, I asked about their issues and was met very quickly with Mr. Know-It-All responses. He had a quip for every turn I took. So I finally asked him this:

- I can see that you have a lot of these issues in good hands. So, what were you hoping to address by having me come here today?

This completely turned the tables. Instead of shooting down everything I said, this question gave him the opportunity to stop attacking and start opening up. At the same time, it acknowledged his need for showing off that he had most of his technology issues already under control.

Some people delude themselves into thinking that the solution they have implemented is the cat's meow. If you know you can offer a better option, use this two-part question set to diffuse a Mr. Know-It-All encounter:

- How is that working out for you?
- Are you getting all of the results you want from that solution?

These questions usually force them to acknowledge their problem areas, giving you the chance to delve deeper into ways you can help. If you have several people in the meeting, you will see some of them bring up topics on their minds.

When you start asking the right questions, people will open up to you because quite often nobody has ever asked them before. This approach allows you to find opportunities and turn prospects into clients by offering ways to make their businesses better. You become a trusted partner, not just a technology vendor.

As you ask these questions, resist the urge to provide a solution after their first response. Continue to ask more questions. Probe to find out what this means to your client in terms of productivity, inefficiencies and other business metrics. Your clients will keep divulging more information with each question you pose. Why? Because everyone has problems they need solved and very few people ask them about it.

Questions are more powerful than answers. The more you ask, the more you learn.

Getting the Testimonial

Client testimonials are a powerful way to spread the word about your happy customers. It also enables you to create case studies that you can share with prospects. One of my clients brings up the idea of doing a testimonial on the first day of his sales process. He lets the client know that getting a testimonial at the end of the project is a key goal for the project team.

Think about what this does: without coming out and saying it, he is communicating up front that he is so confident in his company's ability to deliver results that he is practically expecting them to write a testimonial. That leaves a strong impression in a prospect's mind. You can almost hear their thought process... "Hmm, usually vendors think about asking for a testimonial at the end of a consulting engagement. Here's this guy talking about it before he is even hired. That takes confidence - so he must be good!"

He is consistently impressed with results: clients usually provide a testimonial if his company's technical results are impressive.

Checklist: Your Next Steps

- Train your technical team to sell to your existing clients by offering additional options. What service add-ons can your technicians and customer support reps offer the clients they are in contact with already?

- Brainstorm for a few questions your tech team can ask clients on a regular basis to uncover opportunities waiting to be tapped.

- Refine your questions so they are specific to your clients' needs and the services you offer, and be sure your team is ready to work the questions into their regular correspondence with clients.

PART 3

GO

7

What to Put On Your Website to Hook New Clients

"Let your hook be always cast; in the pool where you least expect it, there will be a fish." - Ovid

"Me" vs. "You" Marketing

Who do you find more interesting? Is it those people who always talk about themselves -- the ones I call "me marketing" folks because their dialogs are all "me, me, me," or those who share information -- the ones I like to call "you marketing" folks because they are genuinely interested in you?

Most of us would rather have a conversation with the "you marketing" folks because they listen to you and offer useful information that can help build your businesses.

Now, translate this concept to companies -- what makes you trust a company you don't know? Those companies who talk about how great they are and what they offer ("me marketers"), or those who put the focus on you without pressuring you ("you marketers")?

This me vs. you dichotomy is being played out on websites all over the Internet. Click through a few sites, and chances are, you'll see a lot of "me" phrases: What *We* Do, *Our* Projects, *Our* Clients, etc. This is considered brochureware. It is content that you might find on a site's "About Us" page, but it doesn't help a prospective client to understand how you can provide solutions to them.

When a prospect can't quickly find exactly what they are looking for they move on and end up working with your competitors. In order to avoid losing potential clients, you must shift your website content from brochureware to expert content. You can easily identify those websites that provide expert content because they are talking about *you*. Expert resources include "you" phrases: What *You* Do, *Your* Goals, *Your* Problems Solved, etc.

In the end, both types of websites make the same statement: We can help you. But, which one would you trust? And, more importantly, which one would you buy from?

In this chapter, I'll cover what makes an effective website. I'll also show you why the best websites focus on the customer by offering expert resources, rather than the company through a brochureware website.

Before we get started with the right things to do with your website, let's take a look at the most common mistakes.

7 Mistakes IT Companies Make with Their Website

In order to shift your company from brochureware to an expert resource, review the following seven mistakes that many IT companies make on their website. If you are finding that you are also falling to these mishaps, you need to make a change quickly.

1. Creating a brochureware website: When a website consists of existing printed materials that have been quickly converted for online use, it is called a *brochureware* website. These websites are not engaging, and they will not result in quality leads or a strong brand.

Today there are plenty of technologies and options available to build a high-quality website that is more effective, but won't break the bank. I'll discuss how to build a website for under $200 later in this chapter. For now, keep the needs of your customers in mind as you write your content. What do they want to read, and how can you deliver it to them to position yourself as a thought leader in your industry?

2. Not providing a clear navigational hierarchy: The best content in the world won't matter at all if your clients can't find it. Use the structure of your site to guide visitors through the valuable information you are providing them. Your home page should clearly explain your goals or objectives (i.e., helping small-to-medium size service companies work in the cloud), and the navigation should be user-friendly. Simply put, don't let your website get in the way of your content or your visitors may not receive your message at all.

3. Lacking in educational material, case studies, or informative content: Like it or not, your website visitors didn't come to your site to learn all about you -- your company history, your client roster, or your accolades. They came to receive useful information that will help solve a problem they are facing.

Create a "Resources" page, and fill it with relevant, accessible information such as white papers, eBooks, instructional manuals, and video demonstrations; these educational materials help you establish trust and authority.

4. Not updating the website regularly with new material: Technologies are changing every day, and new data is always abundant. If you fail to keep up with the trends, or if your content lags behind the most recent studies, your company risks looking irrelevant and out of touch.

Stay on top of industry news and competitive analysis, and incorporate the newest information into your resources. When people view you as their go-to person for breaking news and trends, you will always have their attention. Supplying a constant stream of fresh articles to your blog is a great way to do this.

5. Burying contact information somewhere on the site: Have you ever searched for a company's contact information, only to become frustrated and say, "Why bother?" This is not what you want from your website visitors.

Designate a place on your website to display your contact information, and keep a short version of that information in the footer of every page. Make it easy for visitors to contact you so you can begin building a relationship right away.

6. Not providing a newsletter sign-up form: One of the simplest ways to nurture leads that are not quite sales-ready is through a newsletter. Are you missing out on this opportunity by not including a newsletter sign-up form on your site?

This form of "pull marketing" prompts website visitors to take action to engage with you, rather than in the case of "push marketing," where the company literally pushes its brand through TV and website ads. Integrate a newsletter sign-up form on your site to prompt visitors to seek more information from you.

7. Not taking advantage of search engine optimization: Search engine optimization (SEO) is a competitive arena, but it is critical for IT firms whose entire business is centered around online sales and distribution. SEO helps you stand out from the online crowd by making it easier for customers to find your website.

School yourself in the major tactics involved in SEO. Learn to implement keyword and link strategies, which we will be discussing further along in this chapter.

Upgrading Your Basic Website for Under $200

First a note: not all websites can be done inexpensively. If you build websites and web applications for a living, you know exactly what I mean. Web applications can require significant engineering and creative design work. That said, there *are* some inexpensive options depending on what you are willing to compromise on.

One factor that drives up website costs is custom graphics. This can add thousands of dollars to the price. Unless your core focus is building websites, people typically don't buy technology services from you because your website is pretty; they buy from you because they see you as someone who can solve their problems.

So, unless your website requires an interactive application, a shopping cart or a level of sophistication beyond useful content, why not save yourself some money and just produce great content that portrays you as an expert resource?

Content management system (CMS) WordPress allows you to create a site that you can easily update. You can select from a large collection of free themes or purchase a theme very inexpensively by typing "wordpress themes" into Google to find a myriad of designs. The disadvantage is that the design themes can be used by others who buy the template. However, with this small purchase, you can have all the graphics and structure you need to get your website up and running. Hosting can be very affordable, too. Bluehost offers hosting services starting at a few bucks per month. You just need to fill it with content -- and hopefully with educational content to generate leads.

If your business is to create websites or web applications, then eat your own dog food -- make your site so useful that your prospects wants theirs to be just as effective. Post articles about how to select the best color for links, how much space a logo should take, how to solve a particular anti-aliasing issue with Photoshop, why it is so important to have a contact form above the fold (i.e., visible without scrolling) and other topics that show off your design expertise.

Companies looking for answers to those kinds of questions will seek you out and hire you because you are showing them how to solve their problems.

Why You Don't Get Any Leads from Your Website

If your website hasn't yielded the leads you want, you should start looking at it from your audience's point of view. As previously mentioned, brochureware sites hardly ever attract quality leads because site visitors can't find what they are looking for. But when a site contains useful information that the visitor can actually use, like in expert resource sites, they have a better chance of finding your site and getting what they need.

When a prospect searches on Google, he rarely searches by your company name. Chances are, he will search based on an issue he is facing or a problem that needs solving.

Consider what some of those issues and problems might be. What are the most common issues raised by your prospects and customers? If you are a cloud service provider, your prospects may be searching for "benefits of moving to the cloud," or "how to choose a cloud service provider."

For your website to appear in search results, you'll need to fill it with content that addresses these and other concerns. One way to do this is to write a series of articles on subjects your prospects are interested in. You could write articles on the two topics mentioned above and use them as blog posts, newsletter articles, or even white papers - keep reading.

The point is to create the content your prospects are searching for so they can find you when they need you. Then, qualified leads will start coming to you.

Writing for Clients - and Search Engines

When you write content as an expert resource, it's not enough just to write for clients -- you need to write for search engines, too. Unlike brochureware sites that are often ranked extremely low due to poor quality content, expert resource sites can climb to the top of search engines with the right content and SEO techniques.

Clients are looking for content that is easy to find, easy to digest, and filled with valuable insight that they can apply to their own business. On the other hand, search engines are looking for very specific elements to determine how your site should be ranked.

If you use WordPress, some of the next steps will be done for you because the html code is automatically tagged to be search engine friendly.

Here are three main areas you need to consider when writing web content for search engines:

1. Title Tag: This is the name of your page, which Google uses to see what is on your page. Don't make the mistake of using your company name here; Google will use that to index your page, which won't help customers find you.

Instead, put terms that you want to be indexed for in the title tag. If you provide IT services for doctor's offices, your page might be called, "IT Checklist for Doctor's Offices." Google will know to index your page for these terms, allowing your target audience to find you easily.

2. File Name: Use the same terms from your title tag in your file name.

3. Heading (H1) Tag: Again, use the same terms from the previous two tags in your H1 tag.

When you match all three of these tags, Google really starts to understand what your page is all about, and it will index it accordingly.

Since Google is constantly changing its algorithm, you may want to expand your SEO practices beyond these simple steps to ensure your expert resource website gets noticed by search engines. What we've offered here is what you'll need to do just to get into the game.

When you're brainstorming keywords, think in long tail terms, not just the obvious ones. You'll get fewer searchers, but the ones you get will be very targeted, and therefore, qualified.

For example, don't just stop at "IT services". Go further into the long tail with "IT services for doctors in DC" and the most qualified leads will find you.

Some other keyword rules of thumb include leveraging keyword density to help your page get indexed. Use keywords three to four times throughout the page and make sure the body of the page is at least 250 words because shorter pages usually do not get indexed well.

"dot net" vs. ".net" Example

For this example, I'll be referencing Google's Keyword Tool, which is a free tool that provides a basic sense of what words are being searched for online. This is predominantly used for identify keywords for pay-per-click advertising on Google; however, it can give you some insight into search volume for key phrases as well as finding additional key phrases.

When you use this tool, you'll want to check two columns: In the Competition column, check for terms that are Low, and in the Local Monthly Searches (Local = your country), check for higher numbers.

One way to use the tool is to compare similar terms to see which make the best keywords. For example, if you provide .net services, you may wonder whether to use ".net" with a period, or "dot net" as your keywords.

When you type them into the Google Keyword Tool, you'll see that each of the searches is different, and that more searches have been performed on ".net". However, Google ignores the period before ".net" so it treats it the same as the word "net".

Therefore, the Google Keyword Tool reveals that I should use "dot net" as my keywords to be sure people are searching for the software framework, and not a basketball or butterfly net.

Another way to use the tool is to find variations of your keywords to target. When you scroll down the results in the Keyword Tool, checking for Low Competition and High Local Monthly Searches, you may see that "dot net framework" would make a good keyword candidate, too.

Link strategy

Your link strategy can also help to shift away from a brochureware site by allowing Google to better index your site. When you have a lot of links pointing to your website, Google will assess their authority. If the links are authoritative, Google will elevate your site for the linked term.

Once again, the keywords come into play. If someone links to you, but uses your company name in the link, Google will rank you for your company name -- not your targeted keywords.

One way you can gain links, and ensure they are quality links, is to offer to share information on other people's blogs. If you find a blog that is relevant to your industry, offer to submit a guest post including your keyword links pointing to your site. Now, Google will recognize the links and index you higher for your keywords.

White Papers and eBooks: Perfect for Showing Off Your Expertise

Just like the heading says, white papers and eBooks are the perfect way to illustrate your expertise and separate you even further from a brochureware site. The focus should be on your customer and prospects; how you can help them solve problems they are facing in their own companies. White papers provide an excellent outlet for you to do just that. Plus, it helps you to build trust with your prospects, so that when they are facing a crisis they can turn to you for solutions.

Consider this scenario: Three consultants visit a prospect's office. The first two listen to the problem the prospect is facing, and then say that they understand the requirements, and will prepare a proposal.

However, when the third consultant visits, he offers a white paper to the prospect to read while the consultant is preparing the proposal. This white paper outlines the things the prospect should be considering at this point in the purchase cycle, and it provides useful information to help him make his choice.

Who do you think ends up winning the contract? Most likely, it's the third one because he has proven his expertise, shown he cares about the prospect's problems, and offered valuable content to help the prospect immediately -- simply by giving him a white paper.

Chris Schroeder and his team at App47 understand how white papers can facilitate the decision-making process. Many of the larger companies App47 sells to expect white papers to be part of the marketing mix. So, the company has published two to three white papers in the past 12 months to provide these clients with the in-depth information and case studies they are looking for. Sometimes, calling the white paper an "eBook" instead also works well. Chris finds that some prospects prefer reading an eBook over a white paper.

One of Chris's biggest tips is to be sure you develop your buyer persona well, as I discussed in Chapter 2; otherwise, you'll just be guessing at what kind of audience you're trying to reach and how that audience likes to receive information. In App47's case, white papers proved to be a critical part of the marketing mix, in addition to the newer communication vehicles they use like podcasts and infographics.

Both white papers and eBooks give you the opportunity to show your depth of knowledge on a subject in your industry. They provide the chance to educate prospects so your business will be perceived as an authority in your industry. These tools position you as an advisor to your clients because they learn to trust you. And, when you've built that trust, people will hire you.

How to Write a White Paper

Useful documents like white papers and eBooks don't write themselves. You and your team have the expertise, but may struggle to get started. To overcome this block, one of my colleagues who runs an IT consulting company educates his technical team members on the value of getting the reputation of being "an expert." He points out how others who are viewed as experts in their niche have become well-known, perhaps just locally, and how that led to higher billing rates, higher salaries, more fun work opportunities, fun business travel assignments out of town, and so on.

He encourages his team to write white papers, speak at conferences, develop a short technical class, or run a webinar. And, more importantly, he asks them to brainstorm ways they can distinguish themselves technically. In other words, he asks "what could we invent that could be part of our new 'secret sauce' in one of our niche technologies?" This approach to developing useful educational material has become a very popular side of his corporate culture.

When writing a white paper, it's important to keep the content short and specific. To find a relevant topic for your white paper, come up with the top two or three support questions your clients ask on a regular basis.

These questions will guide you in writing a document on the top issues facing your prospects. When prospects search for information about those issues, they will find your white paper.

Structuring a white paper is fairly straightforward. Here are the sections to include:

- Describe a problem your audience is having.

- Discuss what has been tried to solve that problem.

- Reveal what works best.

- Explain why it works.

- Include your contact information at the end of the paper.

The most important thing to remember is that a white paper is not a sales piece -- it is an educational piece. It is not a brochure, so don't add a hard sales pitch to your readers. Simply including your contact information at the end will help readers get in touch with you. If you sell a product, you can make a small mention of it within the white paper, but don't let it be the focus.

Another way to use a white paper is to build your email newsletter list. Offer the white paper for free in exchange for contact information. Your prospects will learn more about the subject they are interested in through your white paper, and then you can nurture them along with your newsletter.

Form design so people actually contact you

When you offer a free resource on your website, such as a white paper, you'll need a way to collect prospects' contact information. The best way to do this is to create a page with a form on it, often referred to as a "landing page." You can send people to the landing page with a blog article, tweet, or Google Ad, and then offer them the free white paper in exchange for their contact information.

The key to good form design is to keep the form short and sweet. Fewer fields mean more visitors will fill out the form.

So, what information should you ask for? Start with an email address -- this is the most basic component you'll need to keep in touch with a prospect. You can also ask for name and organization and perhaps their phone number and job title (so you can gauge their purchasing authority), but you don't want to push it too far beyond that. The longer the form, the less likely someone will be to complete it. Test variations to see if you get an increase or decrease in the number of completed forms.

You may also gauge a prospect's level of interest by making some of the fields optional. If a prospect is filling out every single field -- phone number included -- that in itself is a self-qualifier.

Tools like Presstacular include a form builder so you can simply copy/paste HTML code onto your website. When someone fills out the form, you are alerted via email, and the prospect receives a link to the material they requested and is added to your email list automatically for future follow up.

When you view a completed form, check their email address. It may reveal just how interested they are in your services. If they provide a Gmail or Yahoo! address, they may not be as serious. But, if they provide a company address, chances are, they are honestly assessing your service for their workplace.

Forms can tell you a lot of useful information, so be sure to get this tactic right.

One final note on form design: Including a picture of an attractive person on your landing page increases the chance that someone will fill it out. The person should be looking out at the visitor, or glancing at the form, to prompt him to take action.

Google Analytics

There are a lot of web analytics tools on the market. Google Analytics is free and does not require much time to setup - there are plenty of books and web articles about this so I won't go into the process in detail in this book. By viewing your analytics regularly, you can see what your visitors find most useful about your site, where they are from and where they leave your site so you can make adjustments to keep them engaged. You can also set up "funnels" to see how your site's flow leads to a visitor completing your contact form.

Google Analytics can be integrated with other promotional tools, such as your email newsletter, so you can see the effect of your email campaigns on website activity.

I've covered a lot of information in this chapter, which hopefully means that you've learned plenty of useful information about making your website great. Some of these strategies take a bit of time and effort to implement, but they can pay huge dividends by bringing targeted, qualified traffic to your website.

Checklist: Your Next Steps

- Go through your website, counting all the "me" words. Could you replace them with "you" words?

- Use the "7 Mistakes IT Companies Make With Their Website" to check that you aren't making any of these costly mistakes.

- Could your website use an upgrade, but you don't have a lot to spend? Check out WordPress, Bluehost, and other low-cost CMS and hosting solutions for yourself. What would it take to revamp your website using these tools?

- Put yourself in the shoes of your prospects. Now, come up with search queries you would use to find services like yours. Better yet, ask someone outside of your industry to come up with some search queries for you. Do you see your keywords among this list? Refine your keywords to a well-targeted and relevant list.

- Check the title tag, file name, and heading tag on each page in your website, using the information I provided above as a guide. Edit these items to include your improved keywords.

- Are you using links effectively as part of your SEO strategy? Make a list of blogs you may want to submit a guest post to.

- Take a look at PRweb.com to see if this service might enhance your press release strategy.

Checklist (continued)

- Are you using white papers and eBooks to position yourself as a knowledge leader? What topics would your prospects and clients be interested in? Brainstorm some ideas for white papers and, possibly, an eBook.

- Go through any forms you have on your site. Edit them according to the form design tips I shared above. Then, test to see if you've gotten it right.

- Add Google Analytics to determine what your website visitors find useful and what bottlenecks may be causing them to leave before filling out your contact form.

8

Blogs: A Key to Social Media Success

"I'm reading a book... if you don't know, it is like a blog except bigger." - Craig Ferguson

It All Begins with Blogs

Blogging isn't just a critical step in your content strategy; it's also the very first step in your social media strategy. Blogs provide a way for you to show off your expertise, get found in search engines and engage in dialogs with people who could become customers. Getting your blog right sets the stage for your entire social media program.

In this chapter, I'll show you how to leverage blogging and social media to transform your online marketing.

Your number one blogging goal should be to publish useful articles on a regular basis so that people searching for information will find you. When deciding what kinds of content to share on your blog, it's helpful to start at the end and move backwards.

What I mean by starting at the end is considering what your target audience will be searching for online. Do they want to know how to use videos to market their products? Are they interested in learning why they should switch to Office 365? Would a checklist of email marketing metrics to track benefit their business?

These are the topics you should cover on your blog. Now, work backwards, actually writing well-researched articles packed with practical information. When your target audience searches for information online, they will find your useful blog articles. And, then, they will find you.

Another benefit of blogging regularly is that it provides a supply of fresh content to use on your other online marketing channels. Consider publishing a highlight reel of your best blog posts once a month in your newsletter.

Be sure to enable comments for your blog so you can engage with readers.

You can also fuel your Twitter stream, Facebook page, and LinkedIn page with content from your blog, which we will discuss in more detail below.

Consider your blog the starting point of your entire content marketing program. When you put time and effort into writing quality blog posts on a regular basis, you will set the stage for success throughout all your online marketing channels.

Business Blogging Success Stories

Let's look at a few companies that blogged their way to success.

Viget

Brian Williams of Viget can attribute $5 million in revenue over the past four years to his blog. That's right -- $5 million.

Viget is a digital agency that creates custom software, platforms for mobile apps, and websites for big-name clients like Puma, Duke University, and the World Wildlife Fund.

Brian and his team began blogging in 2005 with just one blog for the entire company. In 2008, they decided to step things up a bit by expanding to four blogs targeting four different communities: designers, developers, strategists, and marketers. At this point, they ramped up to four to five posts per week total with a content focus on people instead of search engines (however, they did pay attention to which keywords were getting the most traction).

Several high profile clients found Viget through these blog posts as they searched for answers to a technical or design question they were having. Even with clients like Choice Hotels and Time Life, Viget earned their business through blogging, not through salespeople.

Viget receives five to 10 inbound leads each month from its blog and website, resulting in a whopping $5 million in revenue in the four years following mid-2008.

RFID Global Solution

Diana Hage of RFID Global Solution learned the power of leveraging her blog for social media firsthand.

RFID Global Solution is a software and solutions provider focused on enterprise asset tracking, whose primary focus is developing work-in-process tracking solutions for the aerospace industry.

A year ago, Diana started publishing blog posts every two weeks. She gathers contributions from other executives at RFID Global Solution, and she focuses the blog on industry solutions for the company's targeted verticals, as well as upcoming events in the industry.

Diana targets six to eight keywords, which are highly relevant to her niche audience. She is currently testing pay-per-click (PPC) ads to drive traffic to RFID's blog and home page.

Even though she publishes fairly infrequently, Diana makes every blog post count. She connects the company's blog posts to its Twitter and LinkedIn accounts, so that each time a blog is published, a tweet/status update goes out as well.

Diana also leverages her personal LinkedIn account to grow RFID. She has so many LinkedIn connections that the company has closed two deals just from her own LinkedIn network. (More about using LinkedIn in the next chapter)

TRX Systems

Carol Politi of TRX Systems has mastered the art of keyword strategy. Her company has 32 keywords in the top 10 rankings on Google, with 23 ranking in the top three.

TRX Systems develops location systems for tracking public safety, Department of Defense and enterprise personnel in indoor environments, urban areas, and underground -- anywhere that GPS does not work. Their systems also provide after-action reviews for training exercises to show what everyone did throughout the exercise.

Carol and her team began publishing blogs about a year ago, along with search optimized press releases. In a niche market like Carol's, keywords are pretty easy to optimize since there isn't much competition.

TRX Systems began with their five top keywords and used a combination of analysis and guesswork to come up with keywords. They started blogging once every few weeks, sharing company news, awards, job openings, and industry happenings that affected their customers.

Besides blogging, Carol distributed keyword-rich press releases on PR Web to share news on investments, alliances, product releases, contract wins, or other business-centric news.

This keyword-packed content combo has driven inbound leads, especially in the form of distribution partnerships, to TRX Systems. The company averages about six high quality leads per week that convert from the "Contact Us" page on their website.

TRX Systems is enjoying significant success, even though they only post new content every few weeks. They focus on quality, not quantity, with tightly-focused keywords like "personnel tracking," "indoor location system," and "indoor tracking system."

mPortal

Mobile products and services firm, mPortal, has been around for a dozen years. Initially, they did not need to do a lot of marketing because most of their business came from word-of-mouth. Their website was "brochure ware" and they did not have dedicated sales people. In late 2011, CEO DP Venkatesh made a decision to accelerate his marketing efforts to scale up to a higher level of growth.

DP tasked his Senior Director, Azadeh Hardiman, with this goal: position mPortal as a thought leader in the industry. They started by posting two blogs each week, one high-level thought leadership piece from DP and one from an employee to focus on tips and tricks for devices and technical details related to mobile applications.

They didn't just write articles randomly. Instead, they took a methodical approach, focusing on 10 keywords that they felt were critical in their space and another 20 more that they considered to be related. These keywords are terms that prospects might search on. mPortal manually posted a note about each blog to the company's Facebook, Twitter, LinkedIn and Google+ pages to drive additional traffic. This provided an opportunity to add more commentary on the blog and expand their reach.

mPortal took it one step further by publishing white papers to provide prospects with detailed information to help them make buying decisions. They created guides on topics of interest to their clients like HTML5 vs. Native App Development, Social TV and Solving the App Discovery Problem.

After a few months, they added a monthly "wrap up" email which simply previewed the top three highlights they covered over the month and promoted their white papers.

The result: over a period of just eight months, they saw a ten-fold increase in visits to their website. People started filling out their contact form and they have generated hundreds of new leads compared to zero beforehand. Not bad by any stretch!

Network Depot

If you don't see results from your blog immediately, don't worry. That's normal. Network Depot, a managed services provider in Reston, Virginia, was growing at the rate of about 2 or 3 new clients a year. When Vice President and COO Paul Barnett came on board, he wanted to add 2-3 new clients per month.

To generate more leads, Paul enlisted the help of his marketing manager, Robyn Ilsen. She created short videos on the newest version of Windows, ebooks on what to look for when you buy a new computer and other useful resources. Robyn also created a six-month calendar of informational topics to post to their blog. They saw no leads for the first five months. Then, they started getting traction - slowly. They now get about one new lead each week, which they qualify to see if it is worth pursuing.

Keep Focused

Blogging works very well when your article topics align with what your business does and what your audience expects from you. They are not another place for you to post more information about yourself and what your company can do. It is for you to share your knowledge to help solve problems.

Coming up with topics to write about is not as hard as you might think. Network Depot uses Kaseya's remote management and monitoring tool to get alerts when devices go offline, to deploy antivirus software, to perform backups and other services to help manage a client's technology. By looking at how they help existing customers and what kinds of things they need, Paul's team is able to come up with a wide range of topics that their clients and others can use.

Hopefully, these examples have given you some ideas on how to take your own blogging strategy up a notch, and hopefully, they have also inspired you to commit to your blog with regular, helpful articles populated with targeted keywords.

Getting started with blogging isn't that hard. And with a tool like Presstacular, which provides you with monthly content, you can have a rich resource for your clients and prospects almost instantly with very little work (disclosure: this is my company's tool - we built it to address the marketing needs of growing IT services companies).

Be careful of services that provide "fluff" content or material that is not in line with your business. I once saw a blog post on an MSP's website that talked about how to hire a virtual assistant. That's a far cry from virtualization, which is what the MSP specialized in. The blog wasn't doing its job: to show off the company's expertise and position them as a trusted source of reliable IT information. Your messaging should be consistent with the products and services you offer so you attract the kinds of prospects you want, not people looking for secretarial services.

Learn What Your Readers Want

Every quarter, or every month if you publish frequently, look at your blog's analytics to see which posts draw the most visitors. It will give you clear insight into the topics your audience wants to know more about, which can help you craft your product and service offerings.

For a deeper dive into blogs, check out Debbie Weil's *The Corporate Blogging Book.*

In the next chapter, let's take a look at the major social networks that should be on your business's radar.

Checklist: Your Next Steps

- How many articles can you commit to publishing on your blog on a regular basis?

- Who will be responsible for writing, editing, and posting this content? Will you have one team member serve as the staff blogger, or will you ask multiple team members to contribute? Or, would this task be best outsourced to a professional writer?

- What kinds of articles will you publish on your blog? Consider what your target audience wants to know about and will be searching for. Ask your sales team and customer support reps what prospects and clients ask about the most.

- Create an editorial calendar for your blog, as well as a plan for repurposing content on your social media channels.

- Consider trying out a content service like Presstcular that focuses on IT consulting companies to get your content.

9

Social Media: LinkedIn, Twitter, Facebook and More

"When you've got 5 minutes to fill, Twitter is a great way to fill 35 minutes." - Matt Cutts

Social Media: LinkedIn, Twitter, Facebook, and More

With so many social networks to choose from, how do you know which ones to focus on to reach your target audience? This chapter will help you understand how to leverage the most important social networks with social media strategies that get results.

LinkedIn: The Power of Weak Ties

If you work in business, chances are, you use LinkedIn to connect with people in your industry. But, LinkedIn has the potential to connect you with new opportunities and potential leads, if you know how to leverage it.

LinkedIn is the perfect place to harness the power of weak ties. In 1973, Mark Granovetter proposed a theory about social interaction in the *American Journal of Sociology* entitled The Strength of Weak Ties. He believed that the people close to you know about the same opportunities, projects, connections, job openings, and events that you do.

So, to expand your reach beyond your closer circles, you should tap into your other, "weaker" connections to become exposed to a whole new set of options. These mutually beneficial relationships allow you access to what's happening in other circles, while you provide them with access to yours. This is the strength of weak ties.

The easiest and fastest way to strengthen your weak ties is to broaden your LinkedIn connections. If you have not already created an account on LinkedIn, I strongly recommend you do so. Here are your next steps:

- Add the people you know to your network. LinkedIn will then create a list of people it thinks you might know based on mutual contacts. Go through those and add your outer circle to your network, too.

- Get active! As you build your online network, post periodic updates about opportunities you have available as well as those you seek.

- Update your LinkedIn status with links to articles that you find interesting. Others may enjoy them, too. More importantly, they will remember you for posting useful information.

Taking these steps will put you on the radar of your outer circle. If you see a post from a distant colleague that resonates with you, reach out and say hello. Your initiative will leverage your weaker ties and open up new circles of contacts and opportunities.

The day after the last presidential election, I wrote a blog post about how one company used the election buzz to publicize one of their promotions (see *Newsjacking* in Chapter 10). My blog is set to automatically post a status update to my LinkedIn account. The next day, I got a call from a well-known local politician who had seen my status update and wanted to talk about how to leverage my company's technology to win his next election. Although he didn't come out and say my status update is what prompted his call, I knew that is what happened because I saw that he viewed my LinkedIn profile very soon after my post. (Unlike Facebook, you can see who viewed your LinkedIn profile.)

LinkedIn has another tool that can help you identify potential clients and send the names to your inbox. Using LinkedIn's search feature, you can set up and save a set of search criteria and have ongoing search results emailed to you.

If your buyer persona (Chapter 2) guides you to reach people with "CEO" or "Vice President" in their title, who work for healthcare companies, have 500-1000 employees and are located within the Washington, D.C. metro area, you can set up a custom search once and save it.

Every week, you get an email with new people in your LinkedIn network that fit those criteria. Just click on their names to visit their profiles. LinkedIn's upgraded service allows you to send email directly to start a dialog.

Twitter: Now, Even a Customer Support Tool

Many companies are going beyond basic Twitter use to leverage the social network as a customer support tool.

My company, MailerMailer, occasionally receives tweets asking support questions like this:

> How can I post a contact form on my website to get people to sign up for my email list?

One of our staff members sees the tweet and can instantly assist the customer with his question. This kind of instant, personal communication is appreciated by our customers because they don't have to wait for an email response or call in for every question they have.

You can implement a similar approach by regularly monitoring your Twitter feed for customer questions and concerns. A variety of tools can help to make this process easy and efficient.

Hootsuite is an inexpensive solution that tracks keywords among other things. When someone mentions your name (or one of the keywords you've inputted), Hootsuite will notify you via email or smartphone so you can respond quickly.

Other good options for Twitter management include SocialOomph.com and CrowdBooster, which can show you the increase in your follower base and provide analytics on your most popular tweets. You can use this data to compose tweets that resonate most with your audience.

Paul Tomlinson's company, Mirus IT Solutions, tweets about topics that can help a prospect or a client, not information about themselves. They include hash tags, a # sign followed by a word that people can search on to find related tweets, to increase visibility. For example:

> The 25 Most Popular Passwords - If these apply to you, perhaps it's time to change! http://ow.ly/eKLaC #thoughtfortheday

The link directs readers to an article that talks about passwords and the hash tag *#thoughtfortheday* is a popular search string to find related conversations. Mirus also adds personality to their posts, such as things they do for pleasure.

> *#FridayFun Today is a cake day - the Great Mirus Bake-Off is Back! http://ow.ly/hXeie*

This type of post helps Paul reinforce his brand: Mirus is not only a fun place to work, but also a fun company to work with.

You can also include the Twitter handles of other people in your tweets when you refer to something they posted. Since many Twitter users follow mentions of their name, your tweet will show up on their radar. By tweeting something positive about them, you increase the likelihood that they will "follow" you back.

> *The tinned food donations are coming in for @mkfoodbank's Big Little Give this week - good work Team Mirus @Mirusit #biglittlegive*

When you regularly post information that helps others, people pay attention to you when you post a little about yourself:

> *@PT_MirusIT Paul Tomlinson of Mirus IT becomes Founding Member of Kaseya Customer and Partner Advisory Council http://ow.ly/dW5X9*

Mirus was able to build their Twitter connections from zero to almost 500 followers in one year.

Tweeting takes a lot of time. Building an active following means finding content on other sites that you think is interesting and actively pushing out or scheduling 5-10 tweets a day on behalf of your company. If you only tweet once or twice every so often, don't bother tweeting. You will not get much benefit for the time you invest. However, keep your radar out for others who might try to reach you via Twitter.

Facebook: Is it Right for Your Business?

When it comes to marketing to your target audience, you want to be where people are. These days, you can bet that people who might buy your services are on Facebook. But are they looking for services like yours on Facebook?

Creating a Facebook page is quick and straightforward. To get traction, you will need a strategy for getting people to *Like* your page. You may want to offer an incentive or advertise on Facebook itself. When someone *Likes* your page, all of your posts go onto their Facebook news feed, which means you have an opportunity to create another touch point. Include Facebook and other social media icons on your website and email newsletter so people will know how to connect with you.

While some marketers may think Facebook is best suited for business-to-consumer (B2C) companies, many business-to-business (B2B) companies are testing the waters and growing robust communities on Facebook as well. With a B2B page, you shouldn't expect the audience (number of *Likes*) to be as large as a B2C audience simply because there are fewer decision makers as compared to consumers.

Like Twitter, keeping your company's Facebook page updated takes time. The jury is still out on whether having a strong Facebook presence is the best use of time and money for an IT consulting company.

Quora: Your Customers Have Questions, Let Them Know You Have the Answers

Quora is a question and answer network where people post a question, other people respond, and everyone votes on the best answer.

Besides being a useful research tool (you can find out what your customers want to know directly from the customers themselves, so ask thoughtful questions), Quora offers the opportunity to contribute to the community on topics you have expertise in. Be helpful, but don't try to sell. As with other pieces of your content marketing strategy, the goal is to position yourself as a knowledge leader and to genuinely try to help people with their problems.

Quora also serves as a writer's block antidote for bloggers. If you are running out of ideas for your company's blog, check out the questions people are asking that relate to your industry. Be sure to post an abbreviated version as an answer on Quora.

A Quick Note About Pinterest and SlideShare

While Pinterest has gotten plenty of buzz lately, the site obviously lends itself to visually oriented B2C companies. At present, there aren't a lot of case studies showing effective Pinterest use for B2B service companies. At the very least, you may want to check out this popular social media site for reference. If you are limited on time, you might want to skip over experimenting with Pinterest, at least for now.

Another social media sharing tool is SlideShare, now owned by LinkedIn. SlideShare offers a way to share your slide decks to the world. When you produce articles and blog content for your website, the next easiest thing you can do to repurpose the content is to create a slideshow. Post your slideshow to SlideShare along with contact information. The more valuable it is, the higher your chances of pulling in a lead from someone who found your expert information online.

Social Media Does Take Time

Social media is not something you want to begin with gusto, only to abandon in a few weeks when you get busy with other projects. Twitter, Facebook, LinkedIn are all riddled with abandoned social media profiles, so don't let a social media ghost town represent your company online.

If you had to do just one thing, keep your blog fueled with fresh, relevant content. Don't be overly concerned about how much time social media will take. Tools like WordPress can make this pretty easy. When you publish a blog post on WordPress, you can set it to automatically trigger a tweet, Facebook post, and LinkedIn post at the same time your blog appears. Your blog is the starting point from which all other social media flows.

The key to engaging people in all of the different mediums available is to repurpose your content. For example, you could take a single blog article, and transform it into a slide deck, which can be repurposed into a webinar, that when recorded becomes a video. Now, you can publish all of these variations of one single piece of content -- your original blog post -- on LinkedIn, Facebook, and Twitter.

When you repurpose in this way, your blog posts live a long life, and you can share your information with people in the way they prefer to receive it. After all, different people like to absorb information in different ways.

Some of them even prefer to listen to your content, rather than to read it. Chris Schroeder of App47 publishes a podcast called "What's Appening." His audience can download it for free on Chris's iTunes channel and listen to it on their way to work.

When you capitalize on automated technology like this, you'll be amazed at how easily you can reach new people, and therefore, new opportunities, with blogging and social media.

Checklist: Your Next Steps

- Are you leveraging LinkedIn to gain the power of weak ties? Create or update your LinkedIn profile, and start building connections by posting opportunities and helpful information to share with your network.

- Does your company use Twitter for more than just "news flash" tweets? Implement a monitoring strategy so you can assist your customers through Twitter.

- Is your Facebook strategy integrated with your website and newsletter? Create a plan for building your presence on Facebook so you can expand your social media reach.

- Have you tapped into Quora yet? Start using this social network to gather information for blog articles that will get right to the point of your customers' major issues and concerns. Then, consider if you might serve as a valuable advisor on Quora by answering industry-related questions posed by the community.

- Would Pinterest fit into your social media strategy? Consider whether this image-driven network would be worthwhile for your company.

- Take some time to edit and refine your entire social media program. Examine your strategy for each network you participate in, and look at your program as a whole. Are your efforts fully integrated? Are you repurposing content across all channels to create social synergy within all your communities?

10

Email Newsletters: The Ultimate Keep-in-Touch Tool

"Either write something worth reading or do something worth writing." - Benjamin Franklin

Nurturing Leads Till They Are Ready to Buy

I f you aren't using email newsletters to keep in touch with prospects and clients on a regular basis, you are missing out on major opportunities to build trust, establish your company as a thought leader, and -- most importantly -- stay top-of-mind until a prospect is ready to buy.

Email newsletters are the ultimate keep in touch tool because they offer a pressure-free way to communicate with prospects on a continuing basis. Let's say you meet someone at a networking event and you have a nice conversation, exchanging business cards at the end. If this contact is not sales-ready just yet, what do you do?

Instead of just adding her to your customer relationship management database and forgetting about her, you could add her contact information to your email newsletter list. This gives you the opportunity to engage with her regularly, providing helpful information and keeping you top of mind for the particular services you offer.

If you only send her sales pitches, offers or requests to attend your free webinars or lunch-and-learn sessions, she will eventually unsubscribe because the emails are not providing any value. However, when you send her tips, ideas, checklists and other educational pieces that help her business, you build your expert status in her mind.

When she is ready to have a dialog or make a purchase, your company will be on her short list because you have kept in touch and provided valuable knowledge.

Email newsletters are an incredibly effective relationship builder that can lead to real revenue for your company. Many companies, large and small, report that email marketing is their single most important marketing component. It is inexpensive and has a very high impact. Let's take a look at how to get your email marketing program off to a great start.

Who Should You Email?

One of the first things you'll want to know when starting an email marketing campaign is who to send your messages to. Two groups of people that should definitely make your list: contacts that you have met at networking events and your current customers. You can include past clients if you parted on good terms.

What about buying, borrowing, or renting a list? Wouldn't that save you time and effort?

Absolutely not! You should never, ever buy, rent, or borrow an email list -- even if the seller tells you all of the names have opted in to be on the list. The reality is that nobody, not a single person, has ever opted in to be on an email list that is for sale. Think about it. When was the last time you gave someone your email address and said "sure, sell my name and email to anybody?" That never happens. If you use someone else's list, you are setting up yourself and your email service provider for major blacklisting headaches.

Purchased lists also may contain addresses called "spam traps." These may be old or fake addresses that are used to detect if someone is sending unsolicited email. Sending to one of those will get your company put on a blacklist very fast. So, never use third-party lists.

Renting an email list is an option. There are some companies that will do the emailing on your behalf. The ideal way to do this is to find a publication that comprises your target audience. They might have an option for you to buy a "send" to their list.

The best practice for building a genuine email marketing list is to get permission before adding someone. You can do this in a number of ways.

You may want to advertise on the web through a service like Google Adwords, or on a particular website where you know your target audience likes to hang out. When people click on your ad, you usually don't want to send them to your homepage. Unless they see the type of information they are looking for right away, they will leave the page. Instead, send them to a custom landing page -- a page on your website designed to get the reader to take action. Of course, if your home page is designed this way, then by all means use it.

This landing page should include a form to capture visitor's information and allow them to opt into your newsletter. Offer them something in exchange for the opportunity to connect with them through email. You can offer a free white paper on a topic you know they will find useful, or offer a slide deck on a subject that is relevant to their industry.

If you use an email marketing service, like Presstacular, a lot of the work will be done for you. Presstacular automatically creates HTML code for a form that you can copy and paste onto your website to collect contact information from prospects.

At the very least, put a newsletter sign-up form on your website's home page above the fold so nobody has to scroll to see it. You can also put it, or a link to it, on your blog and other content pages so that you can capture contact information from those who find you through web searches.

What Kind of Content Should You Send?

Repurposing
The next thing to decide is the type of content you'll want to send out. You'll find that repurposing will help you get the most out of your content. For example, you may write a checklist on how to select an MSP. This checklist can be posted on your blog, which can be sent via your newsletter article, which can be converted into a slide deck, which can be used for a webinar, which can be recorded as a video, which can be distributed through your iTunes Podcast channel, which can be announced via a Facebook post or a Tweet. So, one piece of content can yield several additional pieces of content in forms that a wide audience can access through their communication channel of choice.

The best subject matter for your content will be useful, relevant information that your audience will care about. Think of ways you can educate your audience so they will learn something new by reading your content, and so they will come away thinking of you as an expert on the subject.

Some examples of articles you can write are:

- Computer Security/Threat Alerts from the Dept. of Homeland Security

- 5 Reasons to Move to the Cloud

- How to Prepare Your Business for the Hurricane Expected This Weekend

- 10 IT Best Practices for Your Doctor's Office

- 6 Simple Ways to Improve Your Website Right Now

- How to Cut IT Costs Without Cutting Quality

Newsjacking

Newsjacking is the process of evaluating the news for stories that have relevance for your customers, and then creating a story based on that news for your blog or newsletter. Read the book, *Newsjacking*, by David Meerman Scott for more details.

Steve Woda of uKnow uses newsjacking weekly to keep in touch with his customers.

uKnow works with organizations to help parents keep their kids safe online by monitoring social media, mobile phones, and location. So, Steve knows that stories about cyberbulling or online safety will really pique the interest of his target audience.

When Steve sees these stories in the news, he makes an infographic to distribute on Vocus or PRWeb. Then, he can share the infographic in uKnow's newsletters, and on its social media channels. Steve provides the added value of keeping his customers informed about issues they care about, and so he remains top-of-mind when his customers seek out online monitoring services for their kids.

Here are some additional ways you can harness newsjacking to create timely articles:

- Write an article about what happens when your staff is out for the holidays, but you need to keep in touch with them. Publish it in December before the holidays, or at the beginning of the summer.

- Publish an article with tips for preparing your business for a storm that the weather forecasters announced is coming.

Writing content that connects with a news story usually gets a high response from your email recipients.

Optimal Emailing Frequency

When it comes to email communication, you should consider testing to see how you readers respond to the frequency of your messages. Once per month is a good pace for staying top-of-mind with customers without overburdening them. mPortal takes summaries of their top blog posts and uses them for their newsletter. It serves as a friendly touch point for their contacts who don't visit their blog regularly. Some companies, who have a lot of information to share and clients who are willing to receive it, do well with two email newsletters per month.

In marketing, there is an axiom that states that it takes seven touches for a prospect to become sales-ready. So, if you're only sending out a newsletter once per quarter, the touch is so infrequent that you may miss out on needs your prospects and customers are having right now. The right frequency can help you stay in their minds so that when the time is right, you'll have already established a relationship.

If you think that sending out an effective newsletter on a regular basis will take too much time and effort, you'll be surprised. Services like Presstacular offer a library of content, attractive templates and custom designs so you can create a polished newsletter with ease.

What to Expect From Your Email Newsletter Strategy

One of the best things about implementing an email marketing strategy is that you can measure your results, which can help you achieve greater efficiency and effectiveness.

Email marketing services offer a wide array of metrics for tracking how many people are opening and clicking on your newsletters. Once you've gained access to this data, you can compare your metrics with other companies to see how well you are doing, see MailerMailer's Email Marketing Metrics Report (you can also search Google for "email marketing metrics"). Track and compare metrics like who opened your message, who clicked on the links in it, and which addresses bounced so you can measure how well your email is performing.

Clever Ways to Use Email Analytics

To get the most from your email analytics, you'll need to take action. Knowing exactly who is engaging with your content can help you work smarter instead of harder.

Suppose you want to reach out to your prospects every few months. Instead of calling everyone on your list, you can use email analytics to hone in on those prospects who are the most sales-ready.

Look through your data and extract the 5 or 10 people who are opening and clicking the most. You will save considerable time and effort if you call these people first since you know they are the most primed to hear your message.

Important: don't call them up right after you see they clicked and say:

> *Hey, I just noticed you clicked on my article about setting up a disaster recovery plan for your business.*

That comes across as creepy. Instead, wait a couple of days and call with a more thoughtful, warm approach like this:

> *Hi Sally, I hope things are going well. I'm calling because we're noticing several companies like yours take a closer look at disaster recovery to protect their assets and I wanted to check in to see if you'd like to explore some options for <name of Sally's company>.*

You know very well that Sally has disaster recovery on her mind. After all, your analytics report shows that she clicked on your link about this topic within minutes of getting your newsletter. By looking at your email metrics reports to see who is opening your newsletter and who is clicking on which links, you learn who your warmest leads are. When you see the same prospects clicking on articles in future newsletters, you will know you should follow up with them quickly. This added interest in your content shows that they are getting close to buying and you can see which type of articles they are reading to help guide your conversation.

Again, avoid the creep factor by resisting the urge to reach out as soon as you notice they've clicked on your email. Wait a couple of days to give them a call so your conversation won't be clouded by a Big Brother vibe.

When you do call, you will be reaching out when you know the prospect is facing a particular problem or issue. Now, you have the chance to become the solution.

If you call and the prospect is still not sales-ready, you can still be helpful. Offer the prospect a tip sheet that talks about things they should be considering or a guide to implementation problems they might face. Use the insight from email analytics to arm yourself with the information you need to nurture the lead or close the sale.

Talk About Yourself, a Little

When you provide educational content on a regular basis, your customers will not mind an occasional marketing message. When you use a two-column newsletter format, you can put an introduction from you followed by article teasers on the left side and information about an upcoming event that you will be at, a new contract you won, staff profile or client testimonial along with contact information on the right side.

Include links that invite recipients to access even more of the helpful resources you offer on your YouTube channel, LinkedIn page or blog. That right column can be used for ads, too. If you offer Office365, include an image that readers can click on to find out more (have the ad link to a page where the reader can fill out a request for a demo). Anyone who clicks on that ad should be called pretty quickly - they are your hottest leads!

Email marketing provides an incredibly effective way to position your company and to communicate with many customers and prospects at once. It offers a way to nurture leads along the sales funnel, and to measure exactly what is working (and what is not) so that you can focus your efforts better and save money. Best of all, it creates an environment in which you can sell to customers who have learned to trust you because they view you as a knowledge leader in your industry.

Checklist: Your Next Steps

- Who will you send your email newsletter to? How will you reach them, and how will you get permission to contact them?

- What kind of content will you send? How can you incorporate repurposing and newsjacking into your strategy?

- How frequently will you send your newsletter?

- How will you measure your email campaigns to see how well they are performing? What specific metrics will you track?

- How will you use the information gained through analytics?

- Create an editorial calendar for your newsletter content, just as you did for your blog. Make sure you have an interesting mix to keep your audience reading. Sprinkle in the occasional marketing message, but be sure it is surrounded by educational messaging so your audience won't opt out.

- Create a free trial on Presstacular to see if it's a good fit for your business.

11

Seminars and Webinars: Knowledge Leader Positioning

"Leadership is influence." - John C. Maxwell

I magine getting 193 leads from just 50 webinar attendees. That's exactly what PR firm SpeakerBox did.

In this chapter, I'll show you how seminars, webinars, and speaking engagements in general can help position you as an expert within your industry, reach new audiences, and create valuable content that can be repurposed for further sharing. I'll also share how SpeakerBox got those 193 leads.

But first, let's take a look at what webinars and seminars can do for you.

Demonstrate Your Expertise

The main value in producing webinars and seminars is the opportunity to demonstrate your expertise to a target audience.

When people attend these events, they are open to learning more about a subject you have considerable knowledge in. That's why webinars and seminars are ideal for positioning your company as a knowledge leader -- your audience is primed to receive the valuable information you are sharing. And companies, like RFID Global Solution, often find that this audience will seek you out for your services once you've gained their trust.

In chapter 8, I introduced you to Diana Hage of RFID Global Solution. Hage and her team have used webinars and good old-fashioned keynote speaking to demonstrate their knowledge in the asset tracking industry.

RFID Global Solution credits the webinars and keynote speaker addresses they give as their most direct sources of lead generation. The company participates in about four of these per year, resulting in around two to three closed deals per webinar, plus about five to six inquiries of interest that they can nurture.

For Hage and her team, producing just four webinars a year has resulted in eight deals with two more pending. Through this one marketing strategy, RFID was able to build the foundation for new qualified leads and successful deals in a way that worked for them.

One of my clients finds a lot of his new business by speaking at technical conferences. He would typically give a demo of some a new system his company had built for a customer, often teaming with the customer to do a joint presentation. He would leave a little time at the end and invite people to come up to the front and talk with the speaker after the presentation.

He found that he would consistently collect more than 20 business cards from people who were worth following up with later. He notes that, although these new contacts were usually technical staff members and did not have direct buying authority, they would convince their senior managers to bring him in for an initial discussion on what his company could do for them using the same technology he had presented at the conference.

Anyone can host an event to build their own foundation for new leads. With seminars, you have quite a few options. You can hold a breakfast meeting, a lunch and learn session, invite people to your office, borrow a conference room from a friend, or even rent out a conference suite in a hotel.

If you would like to reach an audience beyond your geographical location, webinars are the perfect alternative to in-person seminars. Tools like GoToMeeting, Webex and others are available to help you present a professional, worry-free webinar.

Even as few as five to 10 attendees makes for a productive webinar because you have the opportunity to present material to a group of people at once, to interact with them, and to demonstrate your expertise. Recording your webinar for on-demand playback enables you to reach a wider audience.

Preparing your webinar material can be easy, too. For example, if you are a Microsoft solutions provider, you can access free slide decks from Microsoft online to use in your presentation. Perhaps you want to create a webinar on how to set up and use SharePoint.

You can present material on any subject you like and promote your slide deck through Slideshare. To get the word out about your upcoming webinar or seminar, tell people within your partner networks and send an email out to your list (see Chapter 10). You can offer to present a seminar to your Chamber of Commerce or the local branch of your professional society -- or better yet, ones that comprise your target market.

Your presentation can be as short as 15 minutes to an hour for a webinar, or as long as a morning-length seminar.

And, you don't have to go it alone. Perhaps you'll want to organize a seminar with a few other companies. You could serve as the moderator and invite other companies to speak about different topics your audience will be interested in.

For example, if you sell technology services to lawyers, you could invite people who provide other services to the same market. Ask them to serve as a panelist and discuss what trends they are seeing at law practices for using technology to manage billing, customer relationship management or data protection.

Or, on a smaller scale, you could ask someone from your team to moderate for you. You could provide a set of questions to ask, and the team member could interview you.

A good question might be, "What are the top issues law firms face in terms of safeguarding their data?" From there, you might discuss the need to access files remotely, disaster recovery issues, compliance requirements, etc. Talk about your expertise, but be sure to include case studies and examples to keep attendees focused.

Just as I've talked about repurposing other content in previous chapters, you can repurpose your webinars, too.

With a tool like GoToMeeting, you can simply click a button to record your entire webinar. Then, you can post the recording on your YouTube or Vimeo channel, or on your blog, along with the slide deck you created. You can even create an iTunes Podcast channel that people can subscribe to. From there, you can share the webinar on LinkedIn, Facebook, Twitter, and anywhere else you connect with your clients and prospects. Repurposing in this way allows you to get as much mileage as possible from your original webinar.

Provide Solutions to People's Problems

A seminar or webinar is not the time to pitch your business; instead, you should explain how to solve a problem. Your goal is to educate, not to sell. However, your target audience should consist of people you *could* sell to once you've established your expertise.

To find the most pressing problems facing your audience, think about the top two or three concerns your clients raise, and present a 15-minute webinar addressing those concerns.

Create one slide per minute, for a total of 15 slides for the 15-minute webinar, and you'll have a compact, but relevant presentation that tackles the problems your audience is facing.

You can even create several of these in one day, spending about an hour and a half or so, and then trickle them out once a week for an entire month's worth of webinars.

This small investment of time can yield big results, as in SpeakerBox's case. So, let's take a look at how they landed 193 leads from just one webinar.

SpeakerBox Webinar Success Story

Elizabeth Shea, CEO of public relations firm SpeakerBox, created a webinar for their technology clients called "PR 101 for Startups." They announced the webinar to their list and got about 50 people to attend. These attendees yielded several leads.

Next, SpeakerBox repurposed the webinar by posting it on their blog and publicizing it on Facebook, Twitter, and LinkedIn. Within three months, the company got an additional 100 downloads of their webinar. Since SpeakerBox requests contact information prior to downloading the webinar, this translated into 100 new leads.

Then, SpeakerBox got a bonus audience for the webinar it presented months before. One of the people who viewed "PR 101 for Startups" online just happened to be writing an article for the Small Business Association (SBA) about PR, and she linked to SpeakerBox's webinar in her article.

Within the next three months, an additional 93 people found the webinar from the SBA website and downloaded it, giving SpeakerBox even more leads.

Sharing useful, relevant content will drive more leads to your business. You never know what kind of traffic you'll get when you offer valuable content to your audience. In SpeakerBox's case, their high-quality webinar received over 600 views and garnered 193 leads.

Using Web Meetings in Lieu of In-Person Meetings

You can use the same webinar tools to conduct online meetings. Greg Letourneau, CEO of Knowlera Media, a company specializing in video for web distribution and broadcast, leverages webinars and web meetings regularly to communicate with his target market.

Knowlera Media offers a subscription product for TV stations to gain access to unique content without high production costs. Greg says it is cost prohibitive to visit each station in every TV market since there are over 200 of them spread throughout the country.

So, he contacts general managers of local stations to set up a web meeting. This allows him to share his PowerPoint presentation and sample videos without the excessive cost of travel. He uses GoToMeeting as his web meeting tool. Greg is no longer limited by geographical reach. There are other options like Webex, Fuze, Infinite Conferencing and others - all designed for a small business budget.

With some simple technology and preparation, you can present valuable information and answer questions just as effectively as if you were in person.

Webinars, web meetings and live events offer the perfect opportunity to share your expertise and to build trust with your target audience. And, with the tools available today, you can effectively demonstrate your expertise no matter where that audience is located.

Checklist: Your Next Steps

- What topics might your target audience be interested in learning more about? Brainstorm ideas for webinars you could produce.

- Are there any free, readily available resources online that you could use during a webinar (e.g., slide decks)?

- If not, how will you produce the visual component of your presentation? What tools will you use, and who will create this piece of your webinar?

- How will you promote your webinar to be sure your target audience attends?

- What will you say during the webinar, and who will do the talking? Will you use an interview format, host a panel, or deliver a presentation?

- What tools will you use to host your webinar?

- How will you repurpose your webinar content to other marketing channels?

12

What Should Your Marketing Budget Be?

"The key to making money is to stay invested." - Suzi Orman

Think Big and Big Things Will Happen

D o you want to grow beyond $1 million in sales, $2 million, $5 million? Think big and big things will happen. Think small and you will stay small.

As a small business owner, you watch every penny. I remember when I was first starting out, even as sales ramped up, I would watch every penny and try to avoid spending anything on marketing. In the time vs. money equation, I felt my time was cheaper.

I had small sales, so I was reluctant to invest much on anything and relied mostly on word-of-mouth to grow my company. I viewed any cash that went out of the business as an expense, not as an investment.

The result: continued small sales.

I realized I could only grow so much. Word-of-mouth is not a scalable marketing strategy. It is a limiting strategy. I would invest my hard earned cash into stocks and mutual funds thinking those were the right investments to make, even though some of them lost money.

What I didn't take into account was that other people controlled those companies that I was investing in. I didn't have any control over whether they succeeded or not. It was a gamble. Ironically, I had 100% control over my own company and did not invest a lot of my own cash in it.

So, I changed the way I thought about marketing and started looking at options to accelerate growth. The only way to do it was to invest cash for marketing and sales into my own business.

Marketing is an investment, not an expense.

What I'm asking of you is to start by making sure you allocate marketing dollars to invest. Set aside an annual budget, whether it's $2k, $5k, $10k, $50k -- whatever. Just make sure that number isn't zero. Even in 1 or 2 person companies, it should be *at least* $200-300/month if you want to start to grow beyond word-of-mouth.

You can make tremendous strides in lead generation and winning new customers by following the strategies I outlined in this book.

Notice that I did not go into options like trade shows, paid advertising or other high dollar investments. Those are good strategies to explore if you have the budget, especially trade shows - they reach a large number of focused prospects at once.

For this book, I focused primarily on ways for smaller companies, ones with limited budgets, to get the most bang for their buck.

What do all of the activities outlined in this book cost?

Sample Budget

Here is a sample budget on what you should expect to spend.

1. Develop/acquire content: $250-2500/month

2. Articles: included above

3. Blogs: included above

4. Infographics: $200 each (decent designer)

5. Email newsletters: $30-200/month for tool

6. White papers / eBooks: $250-4000 each

7. Slide decks: $100-300 each (decent designer)

8. Webinars: $30-100/month for webinar service

9. Videos: included - just record webinar

10. Podcasts on iTunes: included - just post webinar

Estimated starter marketing budget: $2,500 - $20,000/year (if your annual sales are under $250,000)

Estimated moderate marketing budget: $15,000 - $60,000/year (if your annual sales are $250,000 - $750,000)

Estimated growth-oriented marketing budget: $50,000+/year for every $750,000 to $1 million in annual revenue

These numbers are very general ballparks to give you a sense of what you should consider investing in marketing. Typically, the more you invest in the right forms of marketing, the more awareness you will generate about your company and the more sales you will close.

Start with Educational Content, Then Expand

The core of a small business marketing budget should be educational articles. You can repurpose these in numerous ways with minimal additional effort to access a broader audience. Some prospects will find you from your blog posts, others from your newsletter, yet others from the slide deck you posted as a YouTube video.

Everyone searches for and prefers information in different mediums. With a relatively small investment in reaching prospects in their preferred medium, you easily exceed what word-of-mouth marketing will ever do for you.

As you grow, you may find a need to have more staff to support additional efforts. Consider exhibiting at trade shows that your buyer persona would attend. Online advertising, such as Google AdWords or Bing/Yahoo pay per click (PPC), is also worth exploring -- set aside a $2500+ per month budget for drumming up qualified leads plus more for testing and refining your campaign.

Ads can be directed to landing pages on your website that give away a white paper or eBook in exchange for the prospect's contact information. This will build your email list, giving you the opportunity to nurture and close deals with many companies at once.

Be aware that not every dollar you invest will yield positive results. That's the nature of growing a business.

Don't let a poor return on investment in one area deter you from refining your approach. Stick with it. There is no point starting a marketing initiative only to abandon it after a few months. That's just a waste of money no matter which way you slice it.

Remember, it can take seven contacts or more with a new prospect before they start to recognize your name let alone consider buying something from you. Your newsletter, blog and other content can take a few months or longer to get indexed by Google and your chances of higher ranking go up as you increase your frequency of publishing quality information.

Investing in a focused marketing strategy that centers around the client and refining the bumps as you see the results will give you a clear advantage over your competitors. Why? Because most of them spend their time and money selling, not educating. You can differentiate yourself with your investment: focus on educating and prospects will start to sell themselves.

Checklist: Your Next Steps

- View marketing as a money-making investment, not an expense.

- Allocate an annual marketing budget that corresponds with your annual sales.

- Decide whether it will be easier for you to develop informative articles yourself or acquire them from an outside source that specializes in writing content for your industry.

- Block off an hour or two a each month on your calendar to implement some of the strategies you listed in your budget - make it a recurring meeting with yourself or your partners.

- Bring on consultants or additional part-time help to get things moving if you aren't finding the time to do it yourself.

13

Your IT Marketing Checklist

"Action is the foundational key to all success." - Pablo Picasso

N ow that you have come to the end of this book, I hope
you have gained the knowledge you need to take
actionable steps to grow your business.

To make this even easier for you, I have created a master
checklist that encompasses everything I've covered in this
book. Use it as a guide to get started today on improving your
company's marketing strategy. And, use it to make sure you've

left nothing to be neglected, or less effective than it could be, because every piece of your marketing strategy is important.

Target the Right People:

- Research an audience that is being overlooked, or is currently underserved, that you could offer your knowledge and expertise to.

- Clearly define what you offer, and craft a succinct message to reach that target audience.

- Research the person who makes the final purchasing decision, including their job title and role, and consider how you could help them with the problems or issues they are facing.

- Understand this person's entire sphere of influence, including others in the organization, publications, conferences, or professional associations. Create a strategy for reaching this person; he represents your buyer persona.

Master Your Messaging:

- Review your company's messaging to understand where you are using educational vs. sales messaging. Determine whether these uses are appropriate and make any necessary changes.

- Consider your clients' needs at the Prospect Stage of the buying process, and develop article ideas to meet their needs.

- Next, consider your clients' needs at the Lead Stage of the buying process, and develop article ideas to meet their needs.

- Now, consider your clients' needs at the Opportunity Stage of the buying process, and develop article ideas to meet their needs.

Network Like a Pro:

- Write your elevator speech, including the brief version and the follow-up details. Practice both versions until you have them memorized.

- Review your pricing model so that your clients can see the value you offer. Consider every angle, from packaging your services as a product and positioning yourself as a good outsourcing option, to offering an assessment product or a free, high-value consulting session. Create a pricing sheet to explain what you offer, and at what price, clearly to your clients. Prepare for any pushback you might get.

- Start leveraging your LinkedIn network, as well as your in-person network, to help people find what they're looking for, including: a live lead, a way to make more money, a way to cut costs, a way to save time and increase productivity, and a way to achieve peace of mind. Make a point to scan LinkedIn and other social networks for both business needs and people who could fulfill those needs, on a regular basis.

- Look for organizations to join that are outside your regular network or industry that could get you in front of new prospects. Make a plan to become active in any organizations you join.

- Practice your networking skills, and remember to ask open-ended questions that get people talking about their business needs and the problems they are currently facing.

- Develop your own system for following up with people you meet at networking events, including sending vCards or handwritten notes.

Empower Your Tech Team to Sell:

- Train your technical team to sell to your existing clients by offering additional options. Develop a few questions your tech team can ask clients on a regular basis to uncover opportunities waiting to be tapped.

Make Your Website Work for You:

- Use the "7 Mistakes IT Companies Make With Their Website" to check that you aren't making these costly mistakes.

- Check out WordPress, Bluehost, and other low-cost CMS and hosting solutions to determine whether they could help you upgrade your website on the cheap.

- Edit your list of keywords to include phrases your target audience will be using in their search queries.

- Check the title tag, file name, and Heading tag on each page in your website, and edit them to include your improved keywords.

- Make a list of blogs you may want to submit a guest post to and a timetable for reaching out to them.

- Take a look at PRweb.com to see if this service might enhance your press release strategy.

- Brainstorm some ideas for white papers and, possibly, an ebook.

- Review any forms you have on your site. Edit them according to the form design tips in Chapter 7.

Leverage Your Other Communication Vehicles - Your Blog, Newsletter, and Webinars:

- Create a blog strategy including team members responsible for writing, editing, and publishing posts; post frequency; article ideas based on what your audience is looking for; an editorial calendar to plan your content; and plans for repurposing blog articles.

- Determine who to send your email newsletter to, being sure to address permission issues, frequency, metrics, and actionable steps based on your analytics.

- Decide what content to include in your newsletter; don't forget to leverage your blog content here. You may want to create an editorial calendar for your newsletter content, just as you did for your blog.

- Brainstorm ideas for webinars you could produce. Make a plan for the webinars' production, promotion, and delivery. Consider ways you could repurpose your webinars to get the most from this content.

As you work through this checklist, your marketing strategy will become more targeted, relevant, and effective. Just remember always to view your services from your potential clients' perspectives, and to repurpose all of the valuable content you will create.

And if you need any help along the way, just reach out. See the Appendix on how to connect with me.

Now, it's time take your next step. Go for it! Your business will grow in ways that may surprise you.

APPENDIX

14

Keep Moving Forward

Continue Your Journey

Don't stop now - Make your *IT Marketing Crash Course* experience come alive!

Get access to buyer persona spreadsheets, checklists, webinars, slide decks, white papers, videos, and more – all included as part of your purchase of this IT marketing vehicle. Visit:

www.ITMarketingCrashCourse.com

It will only take a minute of your time and will help you take those next steps as you continue on your *IT Marketing Crash Course* journey.

Partner with an IT Content Pro

Creating valuable, relevant and regular content is hard work, but it is vital to your online marketing strategy. Why not let Presstacular do the heavy-lifting for you?

Presstacular, by MailerMailer, is a next generation email marketing, blog and social media tool that helps IT consulting companies generate warm leads and win more business.

It includes a library of click-and-use technology and business articles, sales letters, alerts and ads created just for IT companies. Every month, you get fresh articles on timely topics that your clients want to know about. Educate your customers on keeping their data secure, moving to the cloud, virtualization and more. You can edit each article to customize it with your own case studies and client examples, or simply use it "as is." Every article you publish instantly becomes part of your blog and seamlessly integrates with your website.

Presstacular has a fully integrated email marketing tool with social media sharing so you don't have to copy/paste anything anywhere. Just point and click to select the articles you want to use, edit them if you want, then press "Send" to distribute your newsletter, sales letter or announcement to your contacts. Live reports show you who is opening your message and clicking on each article or ad so you know who is ready to engage in a dialog with you. It also manages all of the email bounces and subscribe/unsubscribe requests automatically.

Presstacular's email service is whitelisted by all of the major ISPs, ensuring high deliverability of your messages. It includes everything you need to nurture every lead you get: content, templates, tracking. Presstacular keeps you top-of-mind so when clients are ready to buy IT services, they think of you first.

Try it free: *www.presstacular.com*

Need a Speaker for Your Next Webinar or Conference?

Are you hosting a webinar, seminar or conference and looking to help attendees with marketing their technology services or products? I am available to participate as a panelist or feature speaker at your next event.

You can also sponsor this book for distribution at conferences, workshops and seminars or to your customers. Please contact me for options - see contact information that follows.

Let's Stay Connected

What happens if a question pops up while you are implementing the marketing strategies I've covered?

Reach out on Twitter, LinkedIn, or other places around the web, with follow-up questions as you work through the checklists. I look forward to connecting with you! Here's how to reach me:

Twitter:
@RajKhera
@Presstacular
@MailerMailer

LinkedIn:
www.linkedin.com/in/rajkhera
www.linkedin.com/company/mailermailer-llc

Web:
www.presstacular.com
ITMarketingCrashCourse.com

Blogs:
blog.presstacular.com
blog.mailermailer.com
creating-luck.com

Facebook:
www.facebook.com/MailerMailerFan

Amazon:
Did you get actionable ideas from this book? If so, please consider posting a positive review on Amazon. Thank you!